BRICKS & MOR'
stories of Reading bu

Corridor Press is a community publishing project, run mainly by volunteers, which aims to give local people the opportunity to put their words and views into print.

If you would like to get involved in the project, please contact Corridor Press, 21 South Street, Reading, Berks RG1 4QR. Telephone 01734 391029

Bricks & Mortals was published with the support of the Paul Hamlyn Foundation.

Our thanks to Linda Barlow, Tammy Bedford, Tim Bennett-Goodman and Keiren Phelan for their unfailing encouragement and support.

Our gratitude to Kim Chapman of the *Evening Post*, and Manick Govinda of the Paul Hamlyn Foundation, for helping us at crucial stages in the project.

Special thanks go to Reading Girls' School for their enthusiastic support of the project, especially Rosie Bass for coordinating all the illustrations and giving hours of help, and Frances Gregory for organising the writing day.

We also thank Brian Lewis of Yorkshire Art Circus and Christopher Burke for running workshops and providing help and advice; Roy Green, John Rogers and Beryl Pearson for taking photographs; Tony Barham for extra research; Mary Crosier for thinking up the title; Janet Tait for designing the map; and everyone at 21 South Street for their constant support.

This reprint of *Bricks & Mortals* was produced with the financial help of Prudential UK, Reading.

BRICKS & MORTALS

stories of Reading buildings

CORRIDOR PRESS

Published by Corridor Press,
21 South Street,
Reading,
Berks RG14 QR
Telephone 01734 391029

Printed in Great Britain by Antony Rowe Ltd, Bumper's Farm, Chippenham, Wilts, SN14 6QA, England.

ISBN 1 897715 05 6

First published October 1994
Second impression December 1994
Third impression October 1996

Contents

Bouquets & Brickbats: some personal views of Reading buildings

Introduction

Here is a book which has something in it for everyone who lives in Reading whether they have been here a long time or whether they have come here more recently. The former often take their town for granted and play it down, whilst the latter may not yet have got to know it properly.

The book tells us about some of Reading's buildings, such as its once splendid Abbey, its still splendid Town Hall and its prestigious office buildings on the one hand, and its small terraced homes, its back-street pubs and its individual shops on the other. It also tells us about the people who, over the years, lived and worked in them and played their part in the life of the town.

Over 100 people have contributed to the book or played a part in its production, an indication of the reawakening interest that is now being shown in the town. It is an interest that has provided an impetus for the improvements that have recently taken place in the town centre and along its waterways and that causes people to spring to the defence of endangered buildings in areas that they hold in high regard.

It will help Reading to become the kind of town in which everyone can enjoy living.

Molly Casey

Secretary of Caversham and District Residents' Association, a long-standing member of Reading Civic Society, and a renowned conservation campaigner

September 1994

List of contributors

Writers

Tony Barham
John Bird
Nikki Cadd
Rose Cam
William Campbell
Elaine Carthy
Francesca Dendy
Jon Everitt
Mike Facherty
Alison Gibbs
Emma Gibson
Rachel Grigg
Alison Haymonds
Neil Jones
Neal Marsden
Iris Millis
Joan Murphy
Roisin O'Callaghan
Betty O'Rourke
Dermot O'Rourke
Beryl Pearson
Reading Remand Centre
Bernard Redway
Keisha Saunders
Joe Spaguniak
Marion Ward

Contributors

Jean Allison
Elsie Bailey
Jan Bale
Andrew Barker
Angela and Neil Berisford
Nicholas Blandy
Felix Brünner

Bill Cam
Cliff Campbell
Judith Chandler
Dave Charlesworth
Simon Chatterton
Barbara Clifford
Arron and Gavin Cocking
Peter Colebrook
Joanne Cousins
Leslie Cram
Norma Crockett
Jenny Cuff
Peter Dent
Danuta Derczynska
Daphne and Arthur Dewar
Marion Dowling
Patty and Trevor Dunkerley
Tiena Elliott
John Evans
Sue and Graham Evemy
George Fage
Gill Flanagan
Roger Gabbini
Polly Goodman
Philip Goodship
June Gray
Michèle Gray
Dorothy Grugeon
John Hann
Debbie Hawkins
Jo Heald
Freda Izzard
Martin Joseph
Lillian King
Pastor Ahira Lawrence
Laura Milner

Coral Mowbray
Harry Norris
Claire Nurse
Sal Omar
Dot Parish
Dil Patel
Gunvant Patel
Harish Patel
Mahesh Patel
Umakant Patel
Paula Priest
Pupils of Bearwood College
Chris Rogers
Charles Scola
Edith Spencer
Peter Swinn
Brian Taylor
Ivy and Jerry Taylor
Mark Tigwell
Tracey and Michael Turner
Pat Tyler
Anita Villaverde
Tony Ward
Helen Weller
Paul Woodward

Design consultant
Christopher Burke

Cover design
Martin Lacey

Illustrators
Stuart Brodie Thomson
The Design Umbrella
Clive Hacker
Lynne Wilkes

Pupils of Reading Girls' School:
Mehvash Akram
Jacinta Dendy
Tammy Dodsworth
Emma Gibson
Claire Hawkins
Dolina Hussein
Nasreen Irshad
Tahaira Khan
Shakila Mushtaq
Shazia Nighat
Colleen Trushell
Imtiaz Yakhya

Photography
Portraits: Roy Green ARPS
Buildings: John Rogers
Other photos by Beryl Pearson
    and David Portus
Photo of Mrs Dyer: Royal County
    of Berkshire: Library and
    Information Services

Editorial and production
Rosie Bass
William Campbell
Mike Facherty
Alison Gibbs
Emma Gibson
Alison Haymonds
Betty O'Rourke
Beryl Pearson
Jayn Ritchie
Keisha Saunders

Text input
Elinor Dunlop

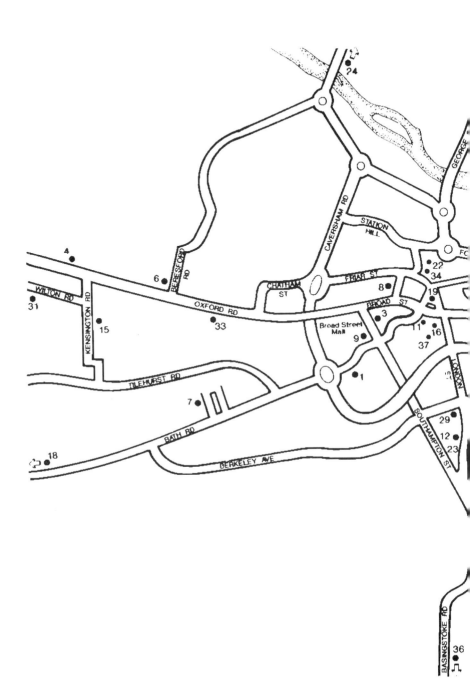

LOCATION OF BUILDINGS
IN BRICKS & MORTALS

Numbers refer to list of contents

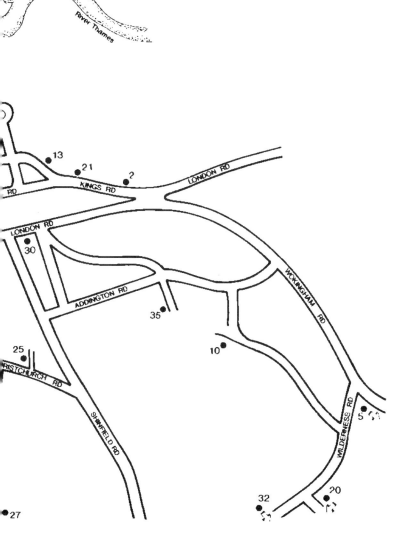

The Almshouses, Castle Street

Charity is not as sweet as it was 130 years ago when the almshouses were built in Castle Street. The houses were originally designed to accommodate 24 'poor people of good character' who had lived in the borough for at least three years. Nowadays it is hard to find residents. 'People become increasingly less willing to accept charity,' says Nicholas Blandy, clerk to the Trustees of Reading General Municipal Charities.

The almshouses were built in 1865 after a number of charities endowed in Reading were consolidated by an Act, on June 28 1861. The Trustees of the newly Consolidated General Almshouse Charities of Reading bought the site in Castle Street, which belonged partly to the charity endowed by a 15th century benefactor, John a'Larder, high steward of the Abbott of Reading. Sixteen almshouses were built for the Almshouse Charities and 12 for the Consolidated Church Almshouse Charities for the sum of £3,961 3s. Another four were added next to the Holy Brook in 1870, for £598 2s 10d, and those 32 remain today.

As time went by, the Church Charities could not afford to maintain their almshouses and eventually, in 1957, the Trustees of the General Charities took them all over under the name Reading General Municipal Charities. The almshouses continue to be run by the Trustees, and the day-to-day administration is the responsibilty of the clerk to the Trustees, and his assistant.

Nicholas Blandy is at least the fifth member of the Blandy family to have been clerk. The Blandys, who have been solicitors in Friar Street, Reading, for more than two centuries, have given unbroken service to the charities for over 100 years, starting with WF (William Frank) Blandy, who died in 1910. He was followed by his son, William Charles Blandy, and then WEM (Ted) Blandy, whose book on the Reading Charities is still in the reference library. His cousin, Peter Blandy, took over from him and about a dozen years ago his son, Nicholas, became the present clerk.

Nicholas Blandy The Trustees became independent of the municipality because local government generally (but not, it appears, Reading Borough Council in particular) had proved to be incompetent at administering charities. There are many more important things for local authorities to do, and it was thought that independent bodies of Trustees were better at doing the job. There are 32 very old almshouses so the Trustees have to keep a careful eye on the routine maintenance of the buildings. Fortunately Reading General

Municipal Charities is well endowed, and at the present time income is in excess of expenditure.

The almshouses have been upgraded in the last five or six years. Recently the Trustees bought a piece of land at the back of the eastern block and built on new kitchens, and central heating has been put in. They are very well built and, despite the steep slope leading down to the Holy Brook, there appears to have been no subsidence. When we built the extension on the almshouse next to the Brook we had to put down special foundations, and they haven't shifted at all.

We used to have only a part-time warden before but people are living so much longer now that the Trustees recently decided to employ a full-time warden for the first time. There are still a lot of almshouses in the country – the National Association of Almshouses is based in Wokingham – and the gap between almshouses and charitable housing associations is becoming increasing blurred. In a Trust like ours, which is relatively well funded, we can afford a warden and proper maintenance, and we can subsidise the rents rather more than some housing associations. Actually residents have a licence rather than a tenancy and they pay a contribution to the maintenance, not rent. We can terminate a licence but it happens extremely rarely. I can't remember it happening.

We actually receive extremely few applications when we have a vacancy in the almshouses, and it is by no means the case that we take only people in the direst straits. Those with the greatest need tend to receive the greatest assistance, and very often it is the people in the middle who come to live here.

We have never failed completely to let an almshouse but we get few replies. It is difficult to understand. These are absolutely ideal places, with a bedroom, a sitting room, kitchen, and a bathroom, and they are in an excellent position, absolutely secure, opposite the police station. There must be some sort of stigma about charity but I find it absolutely bewildering when we have a totally benefit-ridden culture. I think there must have been a change in people's perception of the function of almshouses. They believe it is some sort of religious organisation. Perhaps we should call them something else. We do try to avoid using the word 'almshouses', and we no longer say 'almsperson' but 'resident'.

Regrettably there is a fairly low percentage of male residents because the life expectancy of men tends to be lower than that of women. We have sometimes had sisters and married couples, but by and large residents are single ladies and the average age is well into the 80s. We had one lady, Miss Frankum , who died last year three months after her 100th birthday, and another lady

The Almshouses *drawn by Shakila Mushtaq*

is well into her 90s. There is no pattern to where they come from. They are all individuals.

The Trustees are 16 'competent persons', initially appointed for five years, but the reality is they tend to stay on longer. Many of them are very long-serving, so they know the residents well and visit them regularly.

I think the almshouses, as a group of buildings, are delightful, but of course they have limitations. They are very difficult to heat, the stairs are steep and poky, and they are on a steep hill. Some residents find this a bit difficult and we are putting up a handrail.

Maybe one day we will have to consider moving the whole operation somewhere else to a better-designed building. Of course it would mean a fundamental break with tradition, but change can never be ruled out of the question.

I do enjoy being clerk. It takes me out of the rough and tumble of commercial life for a while. The people involved tend to be nice to deal with. A lot of the residents are very appreciative of the efforts the Trustees make on their behalf, which is pleasing. Yes, I'm pleased and proud to be associated with the charities.

Arthur Hill Pool and Fitness Centre

Pool interior *drawn by Shakila Mushtaq*

The symmetrical red-brick façade can easily be missed exiting at Reading East on the A4. The Arthur Hill Pool and Fitness Centre near Cemetery Junction is a cosy enclave, sporting sashcord windows either side of a polished wood door. A central gable proclaims RSL (Reading Sports and Leisure), part of the Borough Council which owns the pool.

To the left, in the welcoming foyer, a polished plaque displays the origins of the 1911 listed building – Arthur Hill JP, of Erleigh Court, Mayor of Reading from 1883 to 1887. The land was donated by Dr Jamieson B Hurry JP, on the condition it was always used for public purposes.

Michèle Gray and Angela and Neil Berrisford use the pool regularly and they talked about it with duty manager Mark Tigwell.

Mark The place has hardly changed over the years and some of the swimmers have been coming here for 40 years.

Michèle I flirted with various places when I started a get fit campaign but I love this quirky building. Having the changing rooms down the side of the pool is wonderful, it gives the right atmosphere.

Angela Because it's an old place it has certain characteristics. The acoustics are just right and I like the cubicles around the pool. You can get straight into the water.

Neil The staff all know what they're doing here. If you have sports injuries, for instance, they can recommend things to help. I broke my leg playing sports and I found using the gym with the coach was a great way of getting fit.

Michèle At some of the bigger places, something is often missing, but it's human here. The staff all know me by name. The people who come here are all from different walks of life and you could say we had nothing in common. People just know you as a swimmer. It's a great leveller.

Mark
Tigwell

Neil Nobody minds who you are or what you are.

Michèle Some funny things happen. Once I was swimming up and down when this woman said: 'You splashed me, I've just had my hair done.' I could hardly stop myself laughing.

Last year I had a swimming party for my birthday. I hired the pool for an evening for my friends and the regular swimmers I know. The staff put the kids' inflatables in the pool for us, it was wonderful.

People have a real affection for this place.

Mark I've been at Arthur Hill Pool nearly five years now but you never tire of being here – there's such a huge range of activities, yoga, aerobics, circuit training, swimming lessons, gymnastics. There really is something for everyone and the staff work hard to satisfy the different needs of all the users.

Angela At some places you come in, do your bit, then go away. Here people make a real effort. Everybody smiles!

▢ *Brickbat* **VAT Building**

Reading got into a mess in the 50s and 60s. The buildings didn't last because they weren't meant to last. If you look at the VAT building, in Southampton Street, adjacent to the Cambridge Arms, for example, it looks cheap, like the HQ of the Iraqi Secret Police, and is classic mid-60s. It looks as though the architects had a total lack of interest in people.
Jon Everitt

Arthur Prince Betting Shop, The Butts

There can't be many bow-fronted betting shops with a bottle- glass front door. This branch of Arthur Prince still looks from the outside like the cosy tea shop it once was, and people wanting a cuppa still walk in by mistake. The building is old, quite how old no-one is sure, but the Allied Arms pub next door dates from the 16th century. The shop has had a varied history. In the middle of the last century, it was a chemist's, later it became Fred Gomm's basket shop, and then Fenner's sweet shop. The betting shop was only allowed to take over the premises 10 years ago on the understanding that nothing about the appearance of the building was changed.

For its size – and this betting shop is small – it is a very busy one. Probably due to its appearance, more women seem to use it than the many other bookies in the town. It may also have something to do with the helpful staff, who are very used to hearing requests beginning: 'I've never been in a betting shop before. What do I do?' This is especially noticeable just before the Grand National, when business increases several times over. It would seem that a good percentage of the non-betting public has a flutter on the National, if nothing else.

The manager, Roger Gabbini, has many stories to tell about the odd

Arthur Prince betting shop *photo by John Rogers*

things that happen and the unusual characters who come into the shop. Although drink is not allowed on the premises, and the shop is too small for a coffee machine or snack bar like some larger betting shops, there have been incidents with customers coming in from the pub next door, so eager to place a bet they are still clutching their glass of beer. One lady, so inebriated she passed out in the shop, recovered sufficiently to fling her arms round Roger's neck and give him a resounding kiss when he went to her assistance, before drifting off again. Until one of his staff told him, Roger had the lipstick imprint on his cheek.

It was a disappointment to many when the Grand National of 1993 ended in fiasco, but for this betting shop it was a nightmare. Thirteen hundred bets had been taken on the race, and normally all but around 150 winning slips would have been discarded afterwards. But because the race was declared void, every slip had to be checked so that each punter could be given his or her money back.

It isn't just the important events that people bet on, nor are they restricted to national fixtures. A bank of TV sets shows sports not only from all over the country but from Europe and beyond. People bet on races held in Kentucky and in the Caribbean. They bet on beauty contests and whether it will snow on Christmas Day. But the most macabre gambler of all was the man who wanted to place a bet on Nigel Mansell in the Grand Prix. Not to win; this man wanted to put money on him killing himself in the race. The bet was refused.

The Government's decision to allow betting shops to be more open won't, Roger believes, make much difference in practice. There's still a great deal of embarrassment about using a betting shop and punters would prefer the discreet covered windows which conceal them from passers by.

There are many punters who believe they have a system to make money from gambling. There are as many systems as people, ranging from complex computer calculations to studying form assiduously, to backing the favourite in a doubling up system over a series of races. Roger is convinced that none of them is any more reliable than picking whatever takes your fancy, or using the well-tried pin method. There is only one cert, and that is that one cannot beat the bookies for long.

❧ Bouquet The Turk's Head Pub

The place is great. It's very old, timbered in front and with beams inside. At the back there is a new extension where people in black clothes tend to gather. You can look at people in there without them looking at you. It has a mixture of characters – students, someone who looks like a Sioux warrior, and a man who is a BA engineer by day and a barman at night.

Alison Gibbs

Battle Library

Although people in west Reading probably take it for granted, Battle Library is no ordinary building. There cannot be many branch libraries as large and elegant, with busts carved on the gable and stained glass windows displaying the coats of arms of the borough, the Abbey, and its benefactor Andrew Carnegie.

Andrew Barker, supervisor at Battle library for the past four years, said: 'It's a lovely building but I suppose people round here are used to it because it's part of the landscape. It was the first branch library built in Reading when this was the posh end of town. Although Caversham preceded it by a year, that was not within the borough boundary then.'

It was Mr Carnegie, the Scottish-born philanthropist who made his millions as an ironmaster in America, who was responsible for the library's existence. He believed libraries could become 'palaces of delight' and Battle was one of the 660 libraries in Great Britain and Ireland he helped to fund.

At the turn of the century, the population of Reading was increasing so rapidly that the central library, which had been opened at the town hall some 20 years before, was no longer convenient for people living on the outskirts of town, even with the new electric tram lines.

'In such circumstances, the usefulness of the public library and especially of the news and magazine rooms is gradually diminishing, particularly as concerns the working classes who, after a day's work is done, have neither time nor energy to visit an institution at a distance from their homes,' wrote a borough council representative.

In November 1902, the council applied to Mr Carnegie for £10,000 for two libraries in the east end and west end of the town and he offered them £8,000 on the two conditions he always demanded: that a freehold site should be provided, and an additional halfpenny on the rates should be levied for the maintenance of the library.

There was no problem over the first condition. Two sites were bought by Dr Jamieson B Hurry, one in the east end near Cemetery Junction, and the other in the west end, but the second condition proved a stumbling block. The Bill that was promoted in Parliament by Reading Corporation to levy an extra halfpenny rate was defeated.

Enough money was raised by public subscription for one library on the west site but the other could not be built. The site was used for a different kind of recreation, the Arthur Hill swimming pool, and it was not until the 1950s that a branch library was provided in the east end of the town in Palmer Park.

The memorial stone for the new library was laid by the Mayor, Edward Jackson, on October 16, 1907 and a bottle buried in the foundations containing a copy of *The Times* of that day, a local paper, coins and a memento of the borough council.

Jean
Allison

Elsie Bailey, now 92, remembers the library being built, for her father actually worked on its construction. 'My mother was so pleased when we got a library there,' she said. 'She was an educated woman, a pupil teacher, and she enjoyed reading. She used to have to go to into town to get books before that.'

On June 3, 1908, the new West End Public Library and Reading Room was opened by the Rt Hon George Palmer 'with a beautiful key', according to a contemporary newspaper report. Mr Carnegie, who had provided £4,000 for the building, sent his best wishes, and a large crowd of local luminaries admired the Renaissance-style building which was the work of architect Fred W Albury.

The same newspaper reporter described the building as 'simple, dignified and well-proportioned'. It was gaslit (shortened pipes can still be seen hanging down from the ceiling), with lead lights, panelling, elegant arches, and round skylights in the ceiling. Busts of Shakespeare, Newton and Darwin were carved in the front gable as they were considered to be the outstanding men in literature and science. Screen walls separated the various sections but these were removed in 1986 to make the library open plan.

A few years after it was opened, the library was closed again for the duration of the First World War, when it was used as an overflow for Battle Hospital, and in the Second World War it again did service, this time as an ARP (air raid precautions) depot.

Externally the library still looks almost exactly the same as it did nearly 90 years ago but there have been alterations over the years, not least a change of name. It was called Battle Library because the land on which both Battle Hospital and the library were built is part of the Battle Manor estate endowed by William the Conqueror to Battle Abbey after his victory at Hastings in 1066.

Tony Ward

In 1952, the children's library, which occupied the back room on the west side, was screened off, leaded windows were blocked out and that area was taken over by Battle Bindery, the conservation bookbinders, which was set up by the borough to repair and service the bookstock of Reading's six libraries. Tony Ward, who runs the bindery, recalls: 'At the time, some chap said, "They're putting a b... factory in there!"'

The bindery was later transferred to the county council and is now part of the Berkshire Record Office's conservation unit providing a craft and general binding service for the Department of Libraries, Archives and Tourism. In the 80s, it took over the big reading room at the front of the building.

'There was a bit of fuss over that,' Tony recalls. 'They closed it one Friday and moved us in on the Monday – there were a few rumours going round that the library was closing down altogether. The reading room used to be very popular. It had all the daily newspapers and every morning at nine a crowd came in and were settled for the day! If it was raining, they used to dry their coats on the radiators – there were a lot of characters who came in regularly!

'Still, it makes a lovely workshop now and we haven't done any structural alterations at all. We've just recently had it decorated and it looks more like the original than the library itself.'

Battle has always been well used. It is interesting to compare the numbers of books issued 60 years ago, when readers had far fewer distractions, with today. In 1932/33, a total of 60,672 issues was made; last year the figure was 48,264. Of course this does not reflect reduced opening hours and the wider range of services for readers. Andrew Barker says the library is most used now by the two ends of the population – young mothers with new children and retired people.

Jean Allison, who retired in May 1994, after 16 years at the library, knew them all: 'I have seen generations of readers from the very young to the very old. I have watched the little ones grow up and that's been lovely. It's been a bit sad sometimes when the elderly people came in without their partners and I would say to them: "On your own then?" They'd say: "Yes, my husband's not very well ", and I'd ask after them whenever they came in.'

Two of the regular customers, Arthur and Daphne Dewar, a retired couple 'with plenty of time to read', appreciate the library: 'There's a nice atmosphere. We come once a week or once a fortnight on Thursdays, whatever the weather, and always get four books. It's very handy for us, there is plenty of room and it's nice and quiet.'

Battle Library has been through some bad times and a couple of years ago its existence was under threat. However, the library's future looks much more certain now that plans for the development of Battle Hospital site are under way. It seems as though Battle Library could be a palace of delight once again.

Battle Library *drawn by Claire Hawkins*

Bearwood College

The 500 acres of land on which Bearwood College stands, south-east of Reading, was the home of the Walter family which owned The Times *newspaper, founded by the first John Walter at the end of the 18th century. The present house was built by his grandson, John Walter III, MP for Berkshire, and it took nine years between 1865 and 1874. Robert Kerr, an architect, designed Bearwood in a French Renaissance style, and it was built with local labour. The bricks – and there were 4,477,000 of them – were made from clay harvested from the lake and fired in John Walker's own kilns. Oak for the corridors and staircases came from the estate, and carpentry and joinery was carried out in Walker's workshops. The mansion was the last word in Victorian technology, with heating, gas lighting, 22 lavatories, five bathrooms and a saw mill powered by water from the 47-acre lake.*

The Walter family fell upon hard times and by 1919, when The Times *was bought by Lord Northcliffe, the mansion was up for sale. It was then that two ship -owners, Sir Thomas Lane Devitt and Sir Alfred Yarrow, bought it and gave it to the Royal Merchant Navy School. The school was founded in the City of London in 1827 to care for destitute orphan children of British Merchant Seamen and on March 1 1921, it moved into its new home at Bearwood College.*

Entering the grounds of Bearwood, you are dwarfed by the rows of huge Wellingtonia Pines which border each side of the long drive, leading directly to the house. The mansion is heavy with diversely designed pinnacles, towers and chimney stacks.

'It is a beautiful house and I am lucky to work here,' says Jan Bale, who has been at Bearwood for 10 years and worked in every department.

John Hann, who has taught at Bearwood for 35 years, has a more practical view: 'Thick walls make it difficult for the school to make changes and it is very expensive to heat.'

When Mr Hann started it was a school for both boys and girls, but now it is boys only. 'Girls still benefit from the foundation but they have to go to other establishments,' he said. 'After the war, there was no shortage of seamen's orphans but peacetime has appreciably reduced the number. The economic climate has also affected numbers entering Bearwood although we do have pupils from overseas. We could accommodate 500 boys but have only 220 at present. Recently the local paper said that the headmaster was considering reopening the school to girls.'

Bearwood College *illustration by The Design Umbrella*

Another long-serving member of staff is Brian Taylor, housemaster of Jellicoe House, who worked at Bearwood for 25 years then, after a short-lived redundancy, came back for his second stint. His family grew up at Bearwood and one of his daughters was married there.

'It is a wonderful experience to be working here. It is a quiet haven in a sea of suburbia. There is an abundance of wild life, deer, and rare water birds. You are hardly aware that there are housing estates all round. The peace is only disturbed when Concorde flies over.

'When I came here it was a very quiet area, surrounded by country-side and narrow lanes. My journeys to school were eventful. It was a race between me and the herd of cattle. I had to time my departure for school at just the right time otherwise I had to negotiate the muddy lane in competition with cows. If they rubbed against me, I would arrive in the classroom smelling of you know what.

'Jellicoe House was a stable but it became a sanatorium for the Canadian soldiers during the First World War. In the loft, carved in the eaves, are some of the interns' initials and other messages still remain.'

Some of the pupils talked about the school and its ghosts.

Alan I like the old-fashioned and well-kept grounds. It gives you the feel of how it used to be, especially the entrance gates. I like the beauty of South field and the lakes.

James When you first enter the drive you say 'Wow! Look at this place!' It reminds you of some castle. This place has got a lot of history. Everywhere you go you'll find something to do with history.

Muenther I like my dorm. It's like sleeping in your home, except for having a dorm captain, and you don't have your brother and your sister saying 'Keep quiet' every five seconds and telling your mum and dad on you. But I think it would be better if we had private rooms or two or three people sharing.

James There are stories about the ghost of a white maid in the main house. It is said that she fell off the north stairs by the tower and cut herself in three on the circular radiator. No one knows if she was pushed or jumped to her death, but some people claim to have seen her walking up the stairs or heard footsteps near Frobisher Tower.

Another story is about the ghosts of the basements. Apparently these people were practising black magic down there when a faceless ghost dressed in a black cloak appeared. Periodically people claim to have seen this ghost but we went down there and we couldn't find anything.

Muenther There was a plane crash in the lake during the war. They pulled the plane out but the pilot was missing. All they found was a white glove. It is said that one summer's evening three boys went camping by the lake. When the teacher went to check that the boys were all right, he found no one in the tent except a white glove.

Jellicoe was once a stable and they say if you listen carefully at night you can hear a horse coming down the drive. It is said a stable hand was killed by one of his colleagues so the others helped the killer out of trouble by putting the dead man in concrete and using the concrete to build a wall. The story goes that if you are near there at night you can see a white figure where his body was put.

James When my brother came here in 1983, he went to Jellicoe one night and in the dorm they saw the ghost of a sailor. The boys clung together and shouted for the dorm captain. When they went to look, all they saw was liquid where the ghost had been.

13 Beresford Road

For John Bird, 13 Beresford Road in west Reading has a special place in his memory. When he was seven, he went to stay there with his aunt and uncle, Jesse and Minnie Clargo, the first of many visits. Nearly 50 years later, he retraced his footsteps to rediscover the Reading of his childhood.

The war had just ended, and I had never left the shattered landscape of London before. When told I was going to Reading West for a holiday, I felt a mixture of fear and excitement – fear because I had never been away from my parents, excitement because of the adventure of somewhere new.

John Bird

Being only seven, my first impressions were indelible. On leaving the station in the centre of town, I discovered they had weird buses with poles on the top, a bit like trams, but without rails to run on. They made little noise when moving, just occasional clicks – trolley buses. They were not the red and white I thought all buses were painted but a deeper, almost chocolate, colour.

The short journey had other surprises for me. Everywhere I kept seeing 'Co-op'. We had one Co-op store in Peckham, but here there were Co-op shops, milk floats, and bread vans. Perhaps the Co-op owned Reading.

I stayed in a neat, red-bricked house, one of many similar, all in straight rows, off the main Oxford Road, with a new Uncle and Auntie. Everything was different. There were no bomb sites and everything was clean. No emergency water pumps. The terraced house, although small, was warm and friendly. It was spotlessly clean. Auntie took the cleanliness a little too far, I thought, when she scrubbed me clean each night in the scullery at the back of the house. The reward for this suffering was a welcome glass of Corona lemonade. The Corona man called once a week and always got an order from this household.

Next day, my uncle took me to a cycle shop. Not to buy a bike but to get an accumulator charged for the radio. He left one and collected one. This shop fascinated me and in the next week I visited it often, sometimes to look at the bikes, at other times just to see life pass by.

One worker got a contraption out in front of the shop, placed a racing cycle on the rollers and with the help of another, got on the rollers and started racing. He rode like mad to keep his balance. Soon sweat dripped from his nose as he bent over the handlebars. He was training for a race, I suppose.

To the left of the shop, 100 yards or so, was a large railway bridge crossing the road. Steam trains would rush across, full of energy, disturbing the relative quiet of the day. I was soon to learn that Reading was a railway town, and proud to know that my uncle was a steam engine driver. I soon wanted to follow in his footsteps.

To the right of the shop, and a reasonable walk away, was a hospital and army barracks. They were almost opposite each other. Considering the war was only just over, I saw few soldiers, and certainly no American GIs, as in London. I walked until I reached the trolley bus terminus. A man with a pole unhooked the poles on the trolleys from one cable to another in order that they could make the return trip.

Perhaps the highlight of the holiday was walking down Cow Lane to the majestic River Thames. It was not a long walk, passing from a made-up road to a country lane, and then to a footpath. Halfway we went under a wide railway bridge. The river flowed slowly in a purposeful manner. A steam passenger boat, with a flag on the back, puffed by. It was all so different, clean, quiet and with purpose.

Fifty years have passed. Changes abound.

The two most noticable changes when I returned were the absence of Co-op dominance and how cosmopolitan it now is. People from all over the world have arrived and settled. Reading must have a lot to offer for so many to take up residence.

The town has developed with shopping centres, new roads and a new railway station but the railway bridge over Oxford Road still carries trains to London and the South West. The house in Beresford Road still stands much the same as 50 years ago, a little renovated and double glazed. The area has changed though, cars parked on every inch available. Small businesses, car repairs and printers abound.

The cycle shop in Oxford Road has gone, to be replaced by a second-hand furniture store. Battle Hospital is still there but does not look as attractive, with a boom across the entrance stopping cars or lorries visiting. Maybe it is not as important as it used to be? The barracks, further along on the opposite side, is now just for part-time soldiers, the TA, the ATC, and Army Cadets, but it still looks like a great fortress.

Of course, when I got to Tilehurst there was no trolley bus terminal or trolley buses. Returning to Beresford Road, I decided to walk to the river. This was a revelation. Everything seemed at first to change – there is a new roundabout and made-up roads. Where there were allotments and a path leading to a coaling station is now a new red-brick building. On the left side there is a small estate.

The railway bridges have not changed. They are two large brick structures with a narrow single roadway and they have been made safer with traffic lights. As I passed through, I had to look twice to get my bearings. There is now a trading estate as far as you can see.

Beresford Road *drawn by Dolina Hussein*

I had to look in earnest for the path leading to the river but it was there to be found. It has been tarmacked but was a joy to walk on. Birds were singing, the hedges shivered in the wind. It was like walking through a door to another kingdom. The wooden bridge had not altered and old Father Thames at the end of the lane was as majestic as ever.

John made one more visit to 13 Beresford Road and this time he was able to look over the house itself, which had changed little in the intervening years. What is more, Anita Villaverde, who has lived there for the past 15 years, could answer many of his questions about the neighbourhood. Anita, who has worked at a local chemist's for 35 years, was born in Beresford Road, and her grandfather, Mr Chandler, the builder, actually built the houses at the turn of the century. Her mother used to live in Curzon Street and was a friend of John's aunt and uncle. Oddly enough the road was called Beresford Street to start with, but that wasn't considered genteel enough and so it became Beresford Road.

The Chalet, Downshire Square

People who are given directions to The Chalet, in Downshire Square, tend to think they are going to find a little wooden hut instead of the real thing – a building designed on the lines of a Swiss chalet surrounded by traditional Victorian-style houses. Built in the middle of the last century, it is owned by the Methodist Church, who have let it for the past 35 years to the Langley House Trust, a national interdenominational Christian charity, which assists homeless ex-offenders. Social worker Trevor Dunkerley and his wife Patty, who was an architect, have been running The Chalet for 13 years.

Trevor Everybody thinks 'Care in the Community' is a brand new thing; we've been doing it for 35 years here. We still believe in the home emphasis, it's not a hostel. If anything, we are surrogate parents – using social work terms we are in the business of renurturing. Our residents have missed out in their formative years. We provide good, old-fashioned home security, love, friendship, and discipline.

Residents may have suffered past alcohol, drug, mental illness or emotional difficulties – you name it, we accept them right across the board. People tend to stay. After 12 months they may be just beginning to find their feet. Each person has individual needs whether it takes three months or five years. It's about rubbing shoulders, restoring self-worth, and dignity. There's always that open door, like mum and dad saying 'Get out of the nest, but we're here should we be needed'. People come back with their husbands or wives and children 20 years on and say: 'If I hadn't had the chance when I was here, I wouldn't be where I am now.'

People who come here have been through the whole system – homes, approved schools, courts, prisons. If they do something wrong here, their immediate expectation is 'We'll be kicked out'. We try to give them another chance.

We share our home with nine men and three women, all from very mixed backgrounds. Put 12 people from our church together like this and in a few days you'd see the real people coming out.

Working with ex-offenders has special problems. The public has preconceived ideas of what this entails and often declare a NIMBY (Not In My Back Yard) mentality when a new home is proposed. We

The Chalet *drawn by Mehvash Akram*

are part of the community here and we've had nothing but superb relations with our neighbours.

Patty I believe the house was originally built by Sutton himself. He was an alpine seedsman and spent a lot of his time in Switzerland. Someone told me all the land at the back, beyond Brunswick Street cottages, was the original Suttons' Seeds nurseries. Round the corner is the Swiss Cottage public house.

The Chalet has embossed floral work in the plaster at the front. I had the task, when we redecorated, to depict flowers that we'd hardly noticed before. I was going to do it in a coffee and cream type, then thought, 'Oh no, we have the red brickwork'. It could have conjured up a gipsyish look. So I kept it to grey and white and black, and I think that's done the trick.

Trevor Before the Trust took it over 35 years ago, the Chalet was a home for Borstal boys

Patty and Trevor Dunkerley

when Reading Prison was a Borstal. I believe it has been a manse at some time. An old lady in her nineties visited 10 years ago, and said she lived 'under stairs'. Her employer was a Harley Street doctor and this was his country residence. The old lady occupied the cellar, which is now our office and food store.

Doing the garden, I'm always coming across shards of old pots and lots of clay smoking pipes. When they took the footings out for our extension, we uncovered a rather beautiful well. We had absolutely no idea it was there. It is built of Victorian brick, six feet in diameter, with a complete brick domed top. It had to be filled with concrete – tragic really.

There have been lots of alterations; we're always finding bricked-up doorways. The balcony is lead floored. and we spent an awful lot of money to rebuild it. Keeping up to the standard it was when we took it over is quite an expensive job.

The whole of the square has these lovely large lime trees round it. In the autumn, all the trees shed their leaves but one, which retains its leaves for about three or four weeks after the rest have completely shed. It's most peculiar to see. In the spring it is always the first one in leaf. We are certain it is something to do with the roots of this tree going under The Chalet. All the heat and all the love and all the concern that goes on in this place keep that tree going better than the rest.

The Cornish Range, Queen Victoria Street

The local businessman, Charles Fidler, who promoted the construction of Queen Victoria Street at the turn of the century, would probably have admired the enterprise of the brothers who had the bright idea of setting up a Cornish pasty shop in the middle of Reading. Arron and Gavin Cocking started their business, The Cornish Range, after two years travelling the world, surfing and fruit picking. They wanted to create a traditional Cornish bakery in Reading, with all the trimmings – ovens in the shop, milk churns, and an old dresser. They moved into premises previously occupied by Poulters Estate Agents a year ago and now customers can buy traditional pasties, heavy cake, saffron cake and other food instead of houses.

Despite appearances (blond and blue-eyed with a certain laid-back style) they are not Australian but Celts and hail from Helston, near the ends of the earth (well, the UK at least) in Cornwall. The brothers have caused something of a stir among the female population, one smitten customer going so far as to put an advertisement in the Reading University paper saying: 'Any information about the Cornishmen gratefully received. Cash paid.'

The brothers work at the shop six days a week and their opening hours are from 8.45am to 5pm.

The Cornish Range *photo by John Rogers*

Gavin
Cocking

Arron
Cocking

They cook the pasties at 20-minute intervals daily from 7.45am. 'Pasties are a staple food in Cornwall and a way of life,' explained Gavin. 'Pasty shops are as common as fish and chip shops are here.'

So what made them decide to come to Reading? 'We were looking for a town with a large population, but condensed not spread out, and with a sense of community,' said Gavin. 'Word of mouth is essential for a specialist shop like ours. We did consider a London suburb but we felt that community feeling might be missing there. Ideally we wanted a university town with lots of students.'

In the end it was chance that brought them here. In Australia they had met someone from Reading and driving past on the motorway one day, they recognised the name of the town and decided to take a look at it.

'It was daylight when we saw it and very busy, but we have found that at night and on Sundays it is a ghost town,' said Gavin. 'People come here to shop or to work; outside that it is a dead zone. It goes from one extreme to another.'

It proved to be a good time to move into the town because there were a lot of premises available. 'We chose this shop because it was as close as you can get to the town centre without being on the main road and having to pay extortionate rents,' said Gavin.

A Sue Ryder charity shop had been using the premises before the Cockings took over and set about transplanting a piece of Cornwall to Reading. 'You don't need to spend a lot of money,' said Gavin. 'I'm not saying it's a shambles but you can see we've done it all ourselves. People are so used to modern, sterile places, they come past our window and they are mesmerised. I suppose it looks earthy.'

Busy as they are, Arron says they always make time to talk to customers. 'We know our regulars and often have a little chat. On the whole, people in Reading are very friendly.'

The Cornish Range is not a modern shop but it is still not old enough for Gavin.' I hate new buildings and shops,' he said. 'It looks as though Reading tore down lots of old buildings in the 60s and 70s and put up those awful modern ones, all aluminium. What I would really like is a rambling old Tudor building.'

County Delicacies, St Mary's Butts

County Delicacies *drawn by Stuart Brodie Thomson*

County Delicacies Limited, in St Mary's Butts, near The Horn pub, is a unique shop. There is nowhere quite like it in the South of England outside London. If you require authentic Polish ham sausage, German Christmas biscuits or Middle Eastern halva, you will find them here in this shop, not a large one, but crammed with foods from all over Europe and Asia.

Chris Rogers, whose father started the shop in 1950, is a man who lives for his work, and needs to, since he's at the shop from before 7am when it opens, until well after closing time, at 5.30pm, six days a week, but clearly he enjoys doing it.

The shop is a classic example of filling a gap in the market. Chris's father began with a snack bar in Bracknell, but there were problems, so he opened a small delicatessen in Kings Road, Reading, in 1950. In those days, just after the war, there were a large number of Poles and

Ukrainians working in Huntley and Palmer on the night shift. When they left work in the early morning, Mr Rogers' shop was conveniently close and also the only one open at that hour where they could buy food.

It seemed the obvious next step to stock the food they wanted, the kind of foods they were used to in their own countries. There had been a van travelling round the refugee camps selling Eastern European foodstuffs, but the owner was happy to move his stock to Mr Rogers instead.

After 35 years in Kings Road, the shop was transferred to bigger premises in St Mary's Butts in 1985. The shop is always busy and just standing at the door to sniff is a delight in itself, to inhale the wonderful scents of European food.

Chris Rogers may have the only shop where you can find authentic ingredients to recreate that memorable meal you enjoyed on holiday in Israel, or Eastern Europe, but there is another reason for his success, a very individual one. As a result of years working in continental delicatessen in London, where he was often the only English-speaking member of staff, Chris has a fairly good grasp of Polish and German, and often chats to his customers in their own language.

For some of the older generation of Poles, who came to this country just after the war, County Delicacies must seem like a breath of home.

❀ *Bouquet* Queens Road Car Park

I like this building not so much for what it is, but for what it might have been. Instead of a brutishly-designed, stark lump of pre-cast concrete sited dismally in dank, poorly-lit areas, we have a pleasant, horizontal, brick-built façade broken up by simple, vertical, coloured window frames. Above is a traditional-looking grey roof. Inside it is airy and well lit, and it opens out on to an inviting, open stretch of water; a functional building with care taken over its appearance. Thank goodness the council realises now that even car parks can be both safe and aesthetic!

Neal Marsden

Foxhill

Foxhill *drawn by Emma Gibson*

Foxhill lies on the edge of Whiteknights, the campus of Reading University. It was designed and built in 1867 by the best-known architect of the day, Alfred Waterhouse, who also built Reading Town Hall and Reading Grammar School. He intended it for his own use and so, as one might expect, there is something special about the house.

It was designed so that all the main downstairs rooms open out on to a terrace, from which the lawn sweeps down to the lake, which was specially widened at this point to enhance the view. The rooms at the front look out on grounds with mature trees and winding woodland paths which lead to the lake. In Waterhouse's day there was a superb rose garden, considered to be one of the best in the South of England. Recently, the gardens have been restored and the simplified design now provides a peaceful setting for this truly original house.

The brickwork is picked out in a diamond trellis pattern of blue-grey bricks on a terracotta background, and this is continued on all sides of the house and in the stable block. Inside, the panelled library is still as it was when the house was built, and so is the attractive carving on the staircase with its pale tinted glass window on the half landing. In the past 10 years, the university has renovated the house extensively, mainly because of dry rot.

Alfred Waterhouse died in 1905, and the house was acquired by Sir Rufus Isaacs, Reading MP and later Viscount of India. In 1917 it was sold to Lord Hirst, whose daughter was Lady Gamage. This family suffered a double tragedy, Lord Hirst's son dying in 1919 as a result of war injuries, and his grandson, a pilot, being killed in World War Two. Thus Lord Hirst had no heirs, and had it not been for this, perhaps the University might not have acquired the house, along with Whiteknights Park, in 1947.

These days Foxhill houses 40 students as an annexe to Windsor Hall, a next-door modern Hall of Residence. Graham Evemy, the domestic bursar, who has had a flat in Foxhill for 10 years with his wife Sue and their family, says it is lovely living in such a setting, though he regrets that the number of students means that the building suffers a great deal of wear and tear.

No historic house is complete without its ghost, and Foxhill certainly has one, if not several, according to Sue. There is a presence, felt and heard but not seen, who has tapped her on her shoulder, opens doors with a rattle of keys and haunts the cellar. Students say they have heard the jangling of harnesses in the coach house, and there is the mysterious tale of the horsewoman who was decapitated by the bar of a gate when riding into the stables.

Foxhill has other mysteries. Taking a walk round the house with Graham and Sue, one learns that there is more to it than just a beautiful Victorian home. There are puzzles which apparently have no answer.

The staircase window has three panels of pale coloured glass, with three circular leaded lights above. But what is the significance of the symbols on these circles? One is a bat, with wings outstretched, one a half moon, and the other a strange, fish-like creature standing on two legs. Experts say there are three distinct styles incorporated in the windows but are also sure that they are the originals which have been there since the house was built.

The staircase itself is a puzzle, too. The beautiful carved newel post and balustrades have been mentioned in architectural books as original, but there was once a door leading under the stairs to a cloakroom, now bricked up. The height of the door, the outline still visible, would have come above the top of the first flight of stairs. Was this shallow first flight once higher or steeper? In that case, the windows at the top must have reached to the floor. But if that was the case, the plain circles in each of the three panels, convenient now for looking out over the drive, would have been at quite the wrong height.

Rooms have been blocked off, doors sealed and bricked up. While some interior alterations must have been necessary to provide more bedrooms, odd discrepancies in the widths of rooms have been noticed, and the impressive fireplace, a later addition in the entrance hall, is only for decoration. The chimney goes up into the wardrobe of a bedroom.

Foxhill has a fascinating history and one can imagine the Waterhouse, the Isaacs and the Hirst families living here in great comfort over the last 100 years. Now, many more people stay here and enjoy Foxhill. Once the majority of students has departed for the vacation, there are conferences and delegations filling the rooms, the house is often hired for wedding receptions, and foreign students who are not going home, come to stay from other halls which close during the summer.

Foxhill *photo by John Rogers*

The George Hotel, King Street

The George Hotel, standing at the junction of King Street and Minster Street, goes back over five centuries. First recorded in 1423, the building still bears the date 1506 although, 200 years before that, it is thought to have been a coaching inn where travellers stopped for a hot meal and rest on long journeys. The front of the hotel is partly original but the rest of the building is mainly 18th and 19th century.

The inn is said to have been the scene of skirmishes between Roundheads and Cavaliers during the Civil War and is rumoured to be haunted by a Cavalier ghost. In 1747, it was auctioned for £10,400, and in 1914 it officially became an hotel. The saddest event in its long history occurred on May 2 1981, when a devastating fire destroyed one-third of the hotel and killed three people.

The hotel has changed hands many times, particularly in recent years, and is now part of Scottish and Newcastle Breweries. It has also had structural changes and a restaurant, bar, and conference facilities have been added. Most of the people who work in the hotel live in and say it is 'like a big family' and the visitors, mainly businessmen and tourists, love the old world atmosphere and creaky floorboards. Overseas visitors who express an interest in The George can be given an impromptu talk on its background from one of the part-time staff, Marion Dowling, who has always been fascinated by old buildings and their history.

Marion has worked at The George since July 1990. She has also been an assistant manager for Berni Inns in Hartley Wintney and Wokingham, but since she has married and had a baby has worked part-time.

Marion Dowling The first impression you get when you walk in is the courtyard, and with the cobbles and the ivy and wistaria on the walls you can see the place is steeped in history. There are two entrances to the courtyard and you can imagine Roundheads and Cavaliers coming in and having a pitched battle. Legend has it Charles Dickens used this inn as a stopover and he would sit downstairs and write. We still have his chair which we show to visitors. There used to be an old coach outside but unfortunately it was vandalised so we sent it the Museum of English Rural Life.

The courtyard in the autumn months is spectacular when all the leaves turn to gold before they fall. It's my favourite time here. The

The George Hotel *drawn by Emma Gibson*

winter can be quite harsh, because it's an old building and gets a bit whistly round the corridors and a bit leaky in the roof.

The building has been chopped and changed so many times over the years. People who have worked here for a long time can remember what it was like when the restaurant was a coffee shop and the kitchen was in a completely different part of the building. The only thing we're not allowed to touch is the façade because it is listed.

There used to be a fireplace in the middle of the Pickwick Bar and that is where our priest hole was. You can still see the spiral staircase that led up into the bar.

The cellar underneath was linked to what remains of the tunnels that ran under the town and were connected to the Abbey but it's blocked off now. When you go through the hatch into the cellar there are steep steps which are very worn and dangerous. That is one of the reasons we are not allowed to use the cellar any more. It's almost two years since it was used. It hasn't been aired so it wouldn't be very pleasant. I used to go down there sometimes to do stock-taking. The tunnel leads from the part where we used to store spirits. You go round a small corner and it gets narrower and starts heading uphill slightly. You can walk up quite a way before you

Marion
Dowling

reach the bricked-off bit but it's not very high and you
have to stoop.

If you look around the outside of the building, you can
see little squares of glass in the ground which allow light
into the cellars.We actually have five cellars but none of
them reach that far any more.

There used to be sunken shops within the courtyard itself
– there is still a name plaque of one of the old shops. The
new round cobbles laid in concrete block off the old stair-
wells going down into what were the entrances of the shops. In our
boiler rooms underneath the restaurant there are doorways into
rooms with a sheer drop of about 10ft which was how they got the
stock into the storeroom.

The hotel itself isn't actually haunted – I've been in every single
room and there is nothing at all – but in some of the other areas
there is definitely something. It's more an attack of the senses than a
particular sense, a massive awareness, a shiver, all your hair stands
on end. When you know you're on your own in a room and the
adjoining rooms are empty and you hear something, it can be a bit
unnerving.

There is only one part of the building that I won't go into and that
is the Shire Bar cellar. I just won't set foot in there. I am quite sensi-
tive to that sort of thing. No one has actually seen anything, but
there have been accidents down there. One of the managers had a
barrel fall on him, the whole 22 gallons of beer, and that is not the
sort of thing that normally happens. It was quite frightening for him.

The building I work in is very important to me and an old building has more character. I ran a restaurant in a department store once
and there were no windows, no life in that building. It was all
chrome and concrete and I just hated it. I'd much rather be in a
building like this; it lives, it is not just bland.

I am curious about what has changed within buildings. For
instance we haven't any fireplaces left in The George, not one. You
can walk round the building and imagine how things used to be. It's
like a detective story. You don't get a real feel for the place unless
you can talk to people who have known it for years but the stories
that get passed on from living memory are dying out now because
people don't talk to each other any more.

The Greyhound Pub, Mount Pleasant

Mention The Greyhound pub and sooner or later the name of
Bill Mowbray crops up. Although The Greyhound has been
around for at least 400 years and Bill Mowbray ran the pub for
just 19 of them, that period until Bill's untimely death from
leukæmia in May 1990 is remembered as something of a gold-
en age. Bill, his wife Coral, and a group of some of Reading's
most colourful characters made the pub a legend in its own
opening time.

Bill
Mowbray

'People came here for the atmosphere and the landlord,'
explained Martin Joseph, who has been a regular at The Greyhound
since 1978. 'Bill had such a following, he was a real character.'

Martin Joseph worked for Bill at The Greyhound for eight years and
has recently returned to help behind the bar again. Although he still
loves The Greyhound he says it has changed very much since Bill died.
'Bill taught me a lot about how to keep people coming back. The secret
here was to insult them. They'd always come back to see if you were
going to be as rude again. So I've followed the same principle and it does
seem to work.'

One of Bill's closest friends, Peter Swinn, also remembers Bill's individual way with people. 'He had his customers so well trained there
were never any scraps but he did have a unique way of removing people he didn't want in there. He would say, "Sup up or f... off", and if
they acted funny he would down their drink in one. They would look
horrified but go.'

The Greyhound had a hard core of regulars but even occasional customers got a warm welcome. 'Bill had a fantastic memory,' said Coral.
'People could come back to the pub after about four years and "Hi John,
how are you?" he'd say.'

Coral and Bill moved into The Greyhound on November 6 1971. 'We
had our bonfire a day late because there was so much rubbish,' she said.
'We followed Graham Elliott and his wife. Before them the Scearces had
had it for about 125 years. I think it's the third oldest pub in Reading;
only The Sun and The Turk's Head are older. We wanted to make the
pub bigger so we knocked the wall down through to the private quar-
ters and made the extension. There was a working forge at the back and
my husband, who was a keep-fit fanatic, made it into a mini-gym with

a physiotherapist. The physiotherapist moved away and I demolished the gym when my husband died.'

The pub came complete with ghost. 'I've never seen it myself but lots of people say they have seen it,' said Martin. 'It's supposed to have a wide-brimmed hat and it just stands there, usually in Scearce's bar or the cellar.'

Coral never saw the ghost either. She said: 'There was a footprint in the dust but I was still not convinced. I rubbed it away with my foot and it never came back. But animals can tell and my dog Skippy would never go down the cellar.

'Skippy was part corgi, part terrier and he was part of the pub. If you trod on him, he bit you. Customers would say, "Your dog bit me", and I would say, "You started it." Then they would apologise to Skippy.

'Billy Slark grassed the public bar so Skippy wouldn't have to go out in the rain. He brought some turfs in and laid a strip in the bar but Skippy never used it, he was better trained than that.'

Billy Slark was one of the inner circle of locals. Martin said there is reputed to be a mark in the pub still where Billy put his foot against the wall. 'He always used to have one in,' he said. 'No matter what time of the day it was when he came in, it was always paid for. He used to tell tall stories as well. He wound up a couple of students one time telling them he was a Concorde pilot. He had them going for about an hour.'

Peter Swinn also remembered the story of Billy's shoe. 'He had just bought some brand new shoes. He never had new clothes and so the shoes were noticeable. Someone pretended to throw one of them away. He didn't realise it was a joke, went round all day with only one shoe on and then he threw it away. When he got to the pub next day he found the other one nailed to the beam. It stayed there forever – so they say.'

There was another regular called Sid Downer who lived opposite the pub and used to ride through the bar on a racing cycle, or a skateboard, or whatever took his fancy. Sid's wife brought his dinner into the pub one day so he sat down, tucked a napkin in Skippy's collar and they ate the dinner between them.

'Sid was a whisky man,' said Peter. 'On a Saturday we would get him seafood and he would sit and eat jellied eels He would have 10 or 12 double whiskies in a lunch time. In the end Bill would be tipping the jellied eels into the glass with the whisky. We would always get him home but he was so drunk we had to get a taxi and put him in the back seat.

The Greyhound *drawn by Imtiaz Yakhya*

He was driven across Silver Street, got straight out of the taxi and went into his house.'

Peter described the old Greyhound as an élite club. 'There never was any trouble. There was a mixture of young and old – I was probably the youngest in my middle twenties. The average age was 45 or 50. They were all cash dealers such as builders or labourers and there was a great array of backgrounds. Everyone got on and it all stemmed from Bill's attitude. When you walked into the pub you were taken into the fold. We had a great time, it was unique.'

Highlight of those days were the mystery tours. Everyone put 50p a week into a hat until there was a big enough kitty, then the regulars would meet at The Greyhound at 8am on a Saturday morning, Sid Downer would get behind the wheel of the minibus and they would set out for a day's non-stop drinking.

'We left people laughing in our wake wherever we went,' said Peter. 'All of a sudden a dozen of us would arrive in some pub out in the country. They had never seen so many people in one go. If we ordered a dozen pints, by the time the barman had pulled the final pint the first

Peter Swinn (left) and Bill Mowbray *photo by Evening Post*

person had finished his drink, and we ordered another dozen more. I can remember we took on an army tug-of-war team at a local fête – and won! It was only because we had had so much to drink it gave us extra strength.'

Bill's friends were shocked when he contracted leukæmia. 'He never stopped laughing or joking,' said Peter. 'I saw him the day before he died and we had a laugh. It wasn't the same at The Greyhound after Bill died.'

Coral, who now lives in another part of Reading, has fond memories of those days too. 'A lot of sad things happened at the pub but a lot of wonderful things too,' she said. 'After the funeral, so many people came to pay their respects it took me and our daughter Melinda two hours to say "thank you" to them all.

'Bill was a fanatical jazz fan, and he had always wanted to put nothing but jazz music in the jukebox. When the vicar asked us what hymns we wanted, I said: "We don't want hymns, we want jazz." There was jazz when you came in and at the end, after the commital, we played Ella Fitzgerald singing *Every Time We Say Goodbye*. People still say to me, "I heard that song and I thought of Bill".'

❀ *Bouquet* Apex Plaza

Your task, gentlemen:

I want something wonderful, and I want it *smack* in the centre of town. Make it enormous without being threatening, majestic but never boring; draw it so that there's always a new angle that I'd never noticed before.

I want greenery everywhere – on the top, tumbling down the outside, and a whole bloody forest on the inside!

Give me Fun with a capital F – make me smile whenever I see it; I want the architectural equivalent of the Great Pyramid crossed with a bouncy castle. Oh, and one other thing, gentlemen ...

Make it *pink*.

Neil Jones

Huntley and Palmer's

Kings Road

Huntley and Palmer's *drawn by Lynne Wilkes*

The summer of 1994 was the time of the great Huntley and Palmer's debate when the fate of the old building in King's Road was being decided. The biscuit factory was first opened there in 1851, 10 years after Thomas Huntley and George Palmer became partners. By the outbreak of the First World War, the factory had expanded, there were 6,000 employees, and 12 miles of railway track to transport the bisucits. The war changed working life in the factory as Elsie Bailey remembers. Born in 1902, Elsie worked at Huntley and Palmer's when she was still in her teens and she recalls her time there.

Elsie Bailey I was in service in London for two years but then I told them, 'I'm not working for you lot any more', and I came home to Reading. They advertised for somebody at Tilehurst post office, so I worked there for one shilling and sixpence a week, but my friends

Elsie Bailey

Margery and Margaret said I should go to Huntley and Palmer's because I could get 26 shillings there.

I was 16 years old when I went to work in the old building, the one that's been pulled down. We worked from eight in the morning till six at night, six days a week. If you didn't get there by 8am, you were made to sit outside for 15 minutes or half an hour because they wouldn't pay you for that little bit you missed.

We packed biscuits at long benches and we wore old aprons which we had to provide ourselves as there was nothing at the factory. There wasn't much light in there, and we weren't supposed to talk but I sang a bit so the other girls used to ask me to sing. First I packed ginger nuts. They used to rub the skin off your fingers till the blood came through and you couldn't pack any more. Then they let you off for a day or two to do the 'tins', putting the packets in the tins.

I got to be head of the board, in charge of six or eight girls, supervising them to see they were doing the packing, although I didn't get any more money for it. Then they thought I was artistic so I did a bit of icing, putting the patterns on the biscuits.

It was wartime, so there were all girls working in the factory, with just a man running it. Because there weren't any men and I was big and tall enough, they thought I could work in the ovens, putting in the trays. They were big, steel sheets with biscuits on them, and they were so heavy to lift the supervisors used to take me into another room to let me lie down for a bit. But then somebody said: 'No, she shouldn't be doing that', so I got taken off that.

I didn't know what a man looked like until they started coming back from the war. Some of them were in a bad state. You'd see them in the street on little trolleys pulling themselves along. Poor things, it was terrible.

I was at Huntley and Palmer's for two years, then my mother became ill, and I had to stop at home to look after my little brothers and sisters. I was sorry to leave, because I wanted to be back with the girls. After I had finished there, the bosses wouldn't have me back again, so the girls all got together and took me down to the factory and said: 'Look, you're not doing that to her, she can come back.' So they said I could – but I never went back there.

Kendrick View, 39 London Road

The handsome Georgian house, now known as Kendrick View, was the home of Reading's own author, Mary Russell Mitford, and displays a plaque which commemorates this fact. It was also one of the town's earliest dental practices, established before 1891. Built in about 1780, it was still a new red-brick house when Mary's father, a charming but improvident doctor who had spent his wife's fortune in a few years, bought it out of the proceeds of an Irish lottery ticket picked by his daughter. Mary recalls being taken to the lottery office in London by her father on her 10th birthday, December 16, 1797, and insisting on the number 2224. With it she won the huge sum of £20,000 and the Mitfords moved into 39 London Road.

Judith Chandler, *practice manager, has been with the practice for 22 years.* I have probably spent more time in this house than I have in my own home. I came to work here virtually straight from school and I have stayed here ever since with a couple of months off to have my two daughters. I come from Reading, and I knew the house before I came here but I didn't know its history. I think I must have felt it was a very attractive, cosy sort of place and I still feel that. I'd love to be able to buy it and have it for myself.

Judith Chandler

We have many patients who have been coming here for years, some for 50 years or more. One of the first dentists they seem to remember was Guy Ellingham. He planted all the apple trees in the garden. The dentists who came after him were Mr Archibald and Mr Birtwhistle and they were still here when I first came, with James Kirkwood. There are seven dentists now and the longest-serving is Noel Hatton, who joined the practice in 1977. The house used to belong to Reading Borough Council and they let it out to us. Then it was bought by one of the partners in the practice, Steve Noar, and he is our landlord now.

The biggest change to the building took place in 1980 when we had a very bad fire here and the house was completely gutted. We had to move out into Portakabins in the garden whilst the house was being rebuilt inside and it was almost a year before we came back into it.

There is a story that the house is haunted. There are strange happenings and people have heard footsteps overhead. I have never seen anything, but the girls put Christmas decorations up in the small office one year and when we came in on the Monday morning every single one was torn down and ripped to shreds and this started the rumour. It is a good story they relay to new girls.

Jon Heald, *laboratory technician who works in the basement of the house, has personal experience of the 'ghost'.* I haven't heard footsteps for a long long time. It was when I first came here, some eight or nine years ago, and we were doing some work late at night in the workshop. I heard the front door slam upstairs and someone walked across the reception area, as plain as anything, to the top of the little stairs we call the butler's staircase and then walked down to the door at the bottom. I went across to meet him, but the steps stopped so I thought 'He has changed his mind, and gone back upstairs'. I quickly locked up – it only took me a minute – and went out. Total darkness. I thought, 'Hang on, that's strange'. I worked out all the logical, possible explanations and then realised it was absolutely impossible to come in the front door because of the alarm systems.

The girls pull my leg about it but I was absolutely convinced I heard it. I wasn't scared at the time – as far as I was concerned somebody had seen me down here with the light on – and it wasn't until an hour later, when I had driven home to my parents and told them what had happened that it hit me. I can't explain this but I know what I heard. It was strange.

Judith When I first came here, the working day for a dentist was so different. We closed the door for two hours at lunchtime, from 12 until two. Our front door is never closed now from eight in the morning till six at night. I think everybody's working day has got longer which is certainly not what I envisaged 20 years ago. The pace of living has changed. We used to take a morning and an afternoon break and we had a housekeeper who made the tea and put out the biscuits. We don't ever drop the catch now and go down and have a cup of tea together.

Jon It was a classic house with the tradesmen's entrance at the side leading down to the basement, and the butler's staircase so they could answer the main door. I have been told that the extension on the side was the original house and this main building was the

Kendrick View *drawn by Colleen Trushell*

extension. I believe the area at the side of the house was used for sta-
bling and was originally built by Mary Russell Mitford's father.

When I come down the butler's stairs, to the basement where I
work, I can feel three little areas at the bottom, depressions worn by
feet over the years by the staff as they used to come down. It's quite
strange really when you're down here feeling you are in places
where other people have been doing exactly the same years before.

Most of it is original down here in the basement and it is identical
at both ends as though there were two kitchens with an open fireplace and kitchen range either end. There are bells to summon the
servants upstairs and a little cupboard which was a wine cellar. One
of the rooms was a kitchen for preparing meat. There used to be a
huge stone sink here and there's an old meat presser. It is so heavy I
don't know how the heck they got it in here.

Charles Scola, *dentist, joined the practice in 1979 and became a partner in
1980.* I've been a patient here since I was about two years old. My

Charles
Scola

dentist was Mr Birtwhistle who was one of the original partners. My parents were patients and brought me here almost from the day I was born so I have sort of grown up with this building. We used to live in Earley and I took the No 17 trolley bus down Wokingham Road to Jacksons Corner, and walked up London Street, which was a very interesting, bustling street at the time, full of little shops and grocery stores.

I always had fillings and I never understood why, but I loved to see Mr Birtwhistle because he was such a lovely man. He used to call me Little Professor so I thought he was a wonderful character. In my teenage years I used to think 'Well, he's a very happy man and enjoys his job so I want to be a dentist as well.' Really that's how I got into being a dentist because I was inspired by Mr Birtwhistle. So I grew up coming here.

I went to Bristol to do my dental training, and when I couldn't find a partnership in Bristol I applied here, got the job and was offered a partnership. I actually took over Mr Birtwhistle's book. It was a quite extraordinary turn of fate, taking on all the patients of the dentist I used to come to as a child. So after a 10-year break I was back in the same house I used to go to as a child, carrying on the tradition.

Because we have been a practice for so long we get patients who perhaps haven't been to the dentists' for years but always knew there was a dental practice here because they have walked past the door every day. There are about 20 dentists in about five practices in this road – it was a professional road, the Harley Street of Reading.

One of the patients, Harry Norris, now 74, lived in the flat at the top of the house for 16 years when his wife Maisie was housekeeper. Harry first came to Reading in 1951 to find work and was employed at Goodenoughs, the agricultural merchants. He and his wife were sharing a flat in 1953 when they heard about the housekeeper's job from a friend, who worked at Kendrick View as a dental technician.

Harry Norris We applied for the position, my wife Maisie took it over and we moved into the flat. I carried on in my employment and between us we looked after the premises, and the garden. Our daughter, Lynda, was actually born in the house. Our doctor insisted we had enough room in the flat here for 10 babies so he wouldn't sanction her going into hospital. Our room was absolutely inundated with flowers.

We were a bit worried when my wife was expecting Lynda because we thought we might have to move out but Mr Archibald insisted there was no way we would leave or be pushed out, and she got absorbed into the place. Lynda went to St John's school right on the doorstep and there were no problems at all bringing up a daughter here. I was away all day but Maisie was here looking after the staff and house so she was always here when Lynda was on holiday from school. I looked after the garden and my daughter used to sit on the top of the wall and watch the girls from Kendrick School playing tennis. You'd get the smell of the biscuits coming across there from the biscuit factory.

Harry
Norris

We loved the house, my daughter especially so. She was sad to leave. She grew up here and was 12 when we left in 1969, but she still comes back as a patient with her husband and two children.

When we lived here there was a garden room occupying the space where there is now a car park. It was insulated, lovely and warm in the winter, with a wooden floor. I used to play table tennis with my daughter in there. There was an old fireplace with four blue and white tiles either side, each one depicting a Shakespeare play. I don't know what happened to them.

I can remember coming down every morning from our flat and lighting a fire in the waiting room at six o'clock – they've only just taken that fire out. Last time I was here I noticed it was gone. I used to switch Mr Archibald's heaters on, too. We had an Ideal boiler in the kitchen and we were the only ones who used to benefit from that. All our hot water came off that.

Charles It is not a very efficient building in terms of providing dental care, there are too many floors, there are too many old stairways and the rooms are the wrong shape. It's also expensive to run. We thought about moving to a purpose-built, functional clinic which would be more efficient, and more cost-effective, but we would lose that charm and character and we've decided we don't want to do that because patients love the house and we love it too.

45 Kensington Road

The blue front door of 45 Kensington Road is reassuringly bright and normal. There is nothing to make this house, just one in a row of terraced homes, look any different from its neighbours. Yet this was briefly the home of the town's most notorious murderess, Amelia 'Annie' Dyer, known as the Reading Baby Farmer, who was executed at Newgate on June 10, 1896.

Amelia Dyer

The house has changed little in nearly 100 years, according to Michael and Tracey Turner, who have lived at 45 Kensington Road for three years. Michael, 28, who was born and bred in Reading and works at the station as a shunter, looks round the living room and laughs: 'It's a bit of a mess but it's not a frightening house.'

The house must have been quite new when Mrs Dyer moved in. She had come from Bristol, where she had boarded children for many years for a few shillings a month, and arrived in Reading in September 1895, when she advertised that she would board and adopt children. She stayed first in Elm Road, then Piggotts Road, and finally moved into 45 Kensington Road in about February 1896, using the name Mrs Thomas.

It is not a big house and it must have been uncomfortably full when Mrs Dyer moved in with an old lady called Granny Smith, who she had met at Barton Regis workhouse, a lodger called Mrs Chandler, and five children – a nine-year-old boy, Willie, a 10-year-old girl, and three babies. It is hardly surprising that shortly after the motley household arrived, an NSPCC officer came calling and told Mrs Dyer she must register as a baby farmer.

Things got even more uncomfortable when Granny Smith, Mrs Chandler and Willie noticed a terrible smell coming from the kitchen cupboard. Willie later told police he had seen a brown paper parcel in there. The smell disappeared suddenly on March 30, the same day that a parcel was fished out of the Thames at Reading, containing the corpse of a baby girl, strangled with a strong white tape (bought from Heelas) and weighted down with a brick. Three days later two more babies, similarly killed, were thrown into the Thames in a carpet bag.

Mrs Dyer was tracked down to Kensington Road through a former address which she had carelessly left on the first parcel, arrested and charged at Reading Police Station. Eventually seven dead infants were recovered from the river but, although she wrote a confession, she refused to admit how many she had actually done away with, merely saying: 'You'll know all mine by the tape round their necks.'

A Reading woman, Elsie Bailey, who was born only six years after Mrs Dyer was hanged, recalled hearing about the murders when she was a little girl. Elsie, now 92, said: 'It was an awful thing. Mrs Dyer kept on doing away with babies, just like the murderers today. We weren't frightened though. We thought it was part of life, something a bit different. We used to go to the river at Caversham, where Reading Bridge is now – I saw that being built – to see where the bodies were meant to

45 Kensington Road *drawn by Jacinta Dendy*

Michael
Turner

Tracey
Turner

have been taken. We went out of curiosity. I thought that's how life was.'

The history of the house doesn't frighten Michael and Tracey either, even though they are expecting their first baby in October 1994. 'Some people would probably get worried about it but it doesn't really bother me,' says Michael. 'I bought the house from a friend of mine and he'd had two babies before me. When we were buying it, my mother-in-law said "I know that address. There was a woman used to live in there – something to do with babies." She told us a bit about it and there were a couple of articles on the murders in the *Evening Post*.

'Then later my mate was reading a history of Reading and he phoned me up the next day and said, "Here, I'm reading this book and it's got your house in it. Do you know about this?" and I said, "Yeah." "Don't you worry about it?" "No, no".'

Mrs Dyer walked from 45 Kensington Road to the river, carrying her gruesome parcel in a carpet bag. She was seen on the towpath by the Thames on the day the first baby's body was found by a bargeman between Kennet's Mouth and Caversham Lock.

'It's not that far to the river from here,' says Michael. 'You have to go down towards the industrial estate, there's an alleyway cutting through right down to the river, or you can go towards Tilehurst Way.'

Soon after the Turners moved in, they got an unexpected letter through the post. 'Some bloke who used to live in Reading sent us a newspaper cutting about Mrs Dyer,' says Michael.

The man, now living in Norfolk, had written: 'It is not my wish to upset you in any way especially if you are an elderly person and perhaps of a nervous disposition and it is for this reason I have enclosed a separate envelope so that you can open it or throw it away as you wish without reading the contents.'

That was the only time that Tracey was a bit frightened. 'I never got in touch,' said Michael.

No ghost haunts this house. If it did, Michael said he would know. 'I've got a dog and he never worries about anything in here. Dogs normally pick things up before people, don't they?'

Linea, King's Walk

Linea is a hairdresser's owned by Helen and Gary Weller. When the Wellers moved from their old shop in The Arcade to the new King's Walk shopping mall three years ago, it gave Helen a chance to design Linea herself. She has very strong views on shop designs being carried out by people who have personal experience of the business.

When we first moved in, it was just an empty shell. There was nothing there, just bare concrete walls and floor. We actually laid it out ourselves. I think quite often the mistake is having businesses designed by somebody who doesn't actually work in that business, so that a lot of hairdressers look terribly attractive but they are not practical when you actually come to work in them. If you are going to design a hairdressers, it has to be designed by a hairdresser or somebody who knows about hairdressing. I designed the whole thing – my first time. It's a bit scary because you think 'I hope it works' and then when you see it and it does work, it's quite nice.

I think mirrors around the walls are really naff. Separate units give a degree of privacy and the clients feel they are at one with their hairdresser. I think it gives more of an individuality, a separate unit to yourself .

The walls are grey and yellow sponging and the reason I chose yellow is because I thought it looked nice and sunny. Colour is very important especially if you are going to work in it all the time. Something really dark can be very depressing, especially in the wintertime. I once worked in a salon which was chocolate brown and cream and in the middle of winter it was very dark and dingy.

We had a false ceiling put in because the original ceiling was incredibly high. It hides a multitude of spaghetti-junction wires. Everything is up there underneath the ceiling. You take down one of these tiles and it is like a load of knitting wool. The floor is soft, industrial cushion flooring in tile form. You need this because a tiled floor is very bad for your back if you are standing for hours. It has no give in it.

The green work surfaces we actually had made. We had to pick something which didn't show hair too much and didn't show stains. They are made out of wood so they can be painted or restained in a different colour. We can give the salon a new look by simply repainting them.

They are stained and covered with a silicone wax coating to protect the wood from wear and tear.

We have full-length mirrors because I think it is important when you do a hairstyle you don't just design it to a person's face, you do it to fit their body. You have to be able to see somebody full length because faces can be very deceiving. If you have a very small face and a huge expanse of body and you had a very short hair cut, you might look like a cotton bud.

Helen Weller *photo by David Portus*

We have a very silly regulation about the front piece of glass which is fireproofed and toughened. They said we should have a barrier in case a client tried to throw themselves out. They would have to be running at one hell of a speed and they would probably bounce off it anyway. There is just no way anyone is going to fall through it. If you were really suicidal, you would go over the barriers outside.

We outgrew our old shop in The Arcade and when Marks & Spencer closed its doors there and killed the passing trade, it pushed us into moving. We would have liked a ground floor in King's Walk but we needed 1,500 to 1,800 sq ft and we couldn't afford the ground floor rents. The only trouble is, because it is a nice arcade, people tend to be put off and think we will be very expensive but we're not at all. We came three years ago and were among the first. We've seen quite a few people come and go since then. It was nice having the security because where we were before there had been a few thickheads and oddballs wandering about and if the girls were on their own it was quite scary. Here there is security but, like everything, you have to pay for it.

One of my staff, Joanne Cousins, is convinced the shop has a ghost. Some of the girls heard the gown cupboard shut and a couple of spoons drop into cups one evening when they were the only ones there. I've not heard or seen anything at all of this ghost but I'd like to. I was hoping it would come and clean the salon every night!

Lunny's Barn, Tilehurst

A building that now no longer exists was an important part of Marion Ward's childhood The places she remembers – the old barn and the sawmill – have long since gone but when she was growing up, as one of a family of 12, in Reading more than 40 years ago, they were a constant source of pleasure.

When I was a child, we moved to a house in Lyndhurst Road on the Norcot estate. It was 1950 and I was eight years old. My sisters, brothers and I soon found all the best places to play and I think our favourite was a place we called 'The Old Barn'. It really was a barn and it must have been part of the farm which was further up Norcot Road called Minchens farm. Also on this spare ground was a sawmill and the smell of new-sawn wood and the buzz of the saw were just part of the background to our playtimes.

At one end of the barn was a small shed which had been converted into a shop of sorts by a man called Mr Lunn. He always seemed very old to me. What his age was I never did know. I'll always remember his long dirty fingernails and the fag that hung from his mouth, also the smell of the paraffin lamp in the wintertime.

When we were lucky enough to have a penny or halfpenny we would buy a couple of 'specks' from him. These were apples and oranges that were really only fit for the pig bin. Sometimes, though, you could eat more than just a mouthful and these were 'gooduns'.

We always called this little shop 'Lunny's' and it was handy if Mum wanted something that he sold because it saved having to walk further to the shops. Mind you, he always weighed his thumb and all the mud on the potatoes, and Mum said he charged over the top, so we weren't allowed to get the errands there often.

We would take the accumulators to him to be charged and this would cost sixpence. I remember he kept his change in an Oxo tin. My brothers would take empty pop bottles back for a few pence in return. Mr Lunn would put them in a crate round the back and they would retrieve them again and once more get the returns. I don't know how many times this was repeated but I expect that was how my brothers bought their 'specks', so Mr Lunn got his money back in the end.

The other end of the barn was open and inside was an old horse cart which was parked upside down. It had enormous wheels which we

Marion
Ward

would straddle with our arms and legs and then try to beat gravity by clinging tightly and turning in full circle. I don't think I ever achieved it.

There was also lots of spare ground with trees and bushes in which we girls would play. We built camps from old bits of tin or anything we could find. We would make a play table for the dolls and lay it with leaf plates containing blobs of mud and grass for dinner. The dolls were bathed in the muddy puddles when they needed a wash.

On the other side of Lunny's was a round construction which was quite high. The roof was slightly domed – I've learned since that this was a well. The bravest of us would climb to the top and jump off. If you could achieve this feat, you weren't called 'chicken' any more. I plucked up all my courage one day to perform this daring act and nearly knocked myself out as my knees hit my chin when I landed. You can guess, 'chicken' or not, I never did it again.

This whole area was a magic place in the daytime but when it got dark it was the most scary place you could be. The lane that ran by the side of the barn was very narrow and the only light came from one gas lamp. On the other side of the lane was a very high bank which was the side of a cow field. I remember seeing a hedgehog's nest in a big tree trunk which was embedded in the bank. I'll never forget the little babies all pink, bare and blind.

Sometimes when you were walking up the lane in the dark with your heart pounding fit to bursting, you would hear the most scary noise like a heavy breathing and chomping. It would frighten you to death until your mind became logical and you realised it was the cows having a midnight feast. Even then your legs would still become jet propelled.

As I grew older, this magic place became just a part of the local landscape and, after I left school at 15 and had a job that took me away from home, it became an extension of our housing estate for it was sold as part of the farm.

It's strange how open land can bring so much joy when you are young and yet bricks and mortar can do the same when you get older.

The Mansion House

The Mansion House *drawn by Emma Gibson*

The Mansion House, or Prospect Hill House, was built in 1759 by Benjamin Child, who owned the estate which had once been in the Kendrick family. Extended by John Englebert Leibenrood, it was eventually bought by a well-known businessman, Charles Fidler, who was responsible for the council acquiring it in 1901 'for the benefit of weary workers'.

The Mansion House was used as the headquarters for the fire service during both wars, as a tea room, and for football changing rooms. Then it lay derelict for many years until Reading Borough Council entered into an agreement with a catering and brewing company which has now restored it to much of its old splendour and still kept it open for public use. It now has conference rooms, a restaurant, a pub, a manager's flat, a lounge, and banqueting suites.

Stories told and retold from one generation to another become legends. The story of the building of Mansion House is well documented but it is also part of the lives of the people who have lived and worked there. Dave Charlesworth, assistant manager, worked at the Mansion House for three years. This is his version of the Mansion House legend.

There is a romantic story attached to the house. It was built as a private house by Benjamin Child for Frances Kendrick who became his wife. You will know the name of Kendrick from Kendrick School and Kendrick Road. Benjamin had a trade – I believe he was an accountant or he had property or land. Frances Kendrick, however, was one of the high-class, rich people of Reading. I believe the Kendrick family owned most of the land in Reading.

Frances desperately wanted to marry Benjamin Child. The attraction was obviously mutual but he could never approach her because she was rich and came from a different social circle. Benjamin found himself challenged to a duel on Prospect Hill but when he turned up he found out the duel was with Frances Kendrick. Benjamin could not possibly fight with a woman so he paid a forfeit. His forfeit was to marry Frances!

In memory of the occasion, Benjamin built the Mansion House on Prospect Hill on the exact spot that the duel was to have taken place. When Frances died, Benjamin was distraught, so he had a tomb made for her with a stone coffin with her features carved into it. It is believed that the tomb is under the pond which Benjamin also built in memory of his wife. The pond is in the shape of a heart. There is supposedly an underground tunnel leading from the Mansion House to the tomb and Benjamin used to visit his wife daily.

Their names are still remembered. One of the banqueting suites is called the Frances Kendrick Suite and a small conference suite is named after Benjamin Child.

❀ *Bouquet* **Nelson's**

I frequent Nelson's, a wine bar, disco and restaurant carved out of slabs of St Mary's Butts shopping centre at Canal Walk. The cosmopolitan environment and clientele from countries such as Spain, Germany and France appeal to me. It's a quasi-nightclub, with green walls, wooden floors, a dance floor and a small restaurant upstairs. There's no real hassle and it's full of horny people.
Joe Spaguniak, from Cape Cod

Market Place Public Convenience

*The public convenience, right in the centre of the Market Place, must be one of
the oldest of the 17 WCs in Reading, for it was built in about 1933. It is rather
incongruously sited next to the obelisk designed by Sir John Soane in memory
of a former mayor of Reading, Edward Simeon. The WC, still popularly known
as the Butter Market toilet, originally had its walls and floors decorated with
terrazzo work – stone chips set in concrete and then given a smooth surface –
but this disappeared when it was modernised a few years ago. It is now likely
to be closed down and the site used for quite different purposes.*

*Freda Izzard has worked for 21 years cleaning Reading's public conveniences
for Reading Borough Council. Born and brought up in Reading, she now lives
in Tilehurst. She used to work at the Mansion House in Prospect Park and then
became an attendant or 'static' at the Market Place. She now has joined the
mobile team looking after 11 toilets.*

I started at the Butter Market public convenience before they modernised it. It was very, very old but it was nice. In actual fact – a lot of
people might disagree with me – I preferred it as it was. Inside it was
black, even the floors. It was like marble to look at, pebbled with this
special smooth, flint stuff. It used to clean up lovely. They were really
old toilets, they were, but it was a lot better when they were like that.
We used to have the old brass railings coming down. They looked
smashing, especially when the sun was shining. There were even brass
handles on the toilets – they looked nice.

We used to do 'wash and brush up'. We locked off the room and people used to knock and you let them in. We used to have paper towels
and keep it all nice and clean. That vanished, there's nowhere now in
Reading for what they call a wash and brush up. They've done away
with it.

They modernised the Market Place toilet, made it vandal-proof, but
it never turned out right. They altered it, put in fewer toilets – there used
to be a lot more toilets down there – but the water still comes through
the ceiling. They've had it done, spent so many thousands on it and it's
still not right. It's a shame.

People don't use that lavatory as much. They're frightened of it being
underground. Some years ago, before it was modernised, a lady put her
handbag on the floor and somebody followed her down there, put their

Freda
Izzard

hand underneath, got her bag, and went straight up the stairs. Of course you could get underneath the walls then, you can't now because it's blocked off. I asked her why didn't she shout because someone would have heard and she said, 'Oh, I was too frightened.' It's how people are now. We've had people stuck and we've had to climb over. Somebody's tampered with the locks and we've had to go and get a screwdriver and get them out. If you get locked in a toilet it's not very nice at all. Horrible feeling!

It's got very bad, the mugging and different things, particularly in the men's toilets. You get graffiti and you get vandals. It's surprising how much they do. They sometimes take the light fittings out and in Prospect Park toilets they've even wired them from the light to the door. Anybody going in would get a nasty shock. We've gone very careful and locked it up and called the electricians out.

You get naughty drawings. There's one that keeps appearing every so often, a complete drawing. He must spend hours in there, it's massive. It's a drawing of a nude woman, all in colour with all the details. It's really artistic. Sally Fraser we call her. The boys always say: 'Sally Fraser's been around.' We've got a new name for her now, Sue Davis. It's right along by the urinals. You can see it's the same person who's doing it, it's the same shapes. It's been at Whitley Street, and down the Prom, Wilson Road, and the White House.

You usually get the girls leaving messages for another girl. 'See you at 9 o'clock tonight', something like that. Sometimes it's obscene. You get that off yourself but if it's too much the graffiti team comes in. They use friendly green chemicals.

You get the drunks that come in at different times, people that have drinking problems, sickness which you just accept. You don't get on to them or you're asking for trouble.

You are only doing a service. Some people say, 'Ugh, I wouldn't want to work there', but to me it's a very satisfactory job. You see all different kinds of things going on and you come into contact with the public.

I like it, or I wouldn't have stayed here for 21 years.

Mobile Information Centre, Earley

The Mobile Information Centre serves in place of a building. It is parked in the Asda car park at Earley on Wednesdays and Thursdays from 10am to 4pm. It's a grand name for a caravan which has seen better days but, brightly painted and covered in leaflets and posters inside and out, it is a mobile mine of information on anything from health to benefits, leisure facilities to bus times. It's there in all weathers. If it rains, Lillian King and her volunteer helpers have to rush out with sheets of plastic to cover the leaflets; if the sun shines, they sit outside in deckchairs. Only the wind drives them away.

Lillian King, *part-time project co-ordinator.* About six years ago, as Lower Earley was developing, a group of concerned Earley residents got together because they could see that the development was happening and there were no community resources – it's the largest private housing estate in Europe, although Woodley is coming close! So they had a public meeting and decided the most useful thing would be access to information so that people new to the area would know where they could go for help.

Lillian King

People were experiencing problems of not having any kind of identity in the neighbourhood because everybody was new, and there wasn't an established community to ask about these things. You need to know when the dustbin day is, when the library is open, and so on. The caravan idea was thought of because it could move around the various little localities offering support. There weren't any permanent community buildings available then.

Gill Flanagan, *community resource worker for Earley.* I was Community Development Worker with Social Services and was working with the group. We had agreed Social Services were going to fund the purchase of the caravan and I had tentatively begun to look around when, one Sunday afternoon, I was visiting friends in North Ascot and there it was, outside someone's house, with a 'For Sale' sign on it. So I just knocked on the door and the elderly couple who lived there were so nice and gave me tea.

This was very much a family caravan. They had had a lot of adventures in it and were rather loath to part with it but they were really keen to sell to us as it was going to a good home. I can't remember how much we paid – about £700. It was fairly well used then and we have had it now for six years.

So we hitched it up and towed it home. People were a bit suspicious at first and thought we were double glazing so we had it painted in wonderful rainbow stripes which made people identify us. It has done extremely well. It is an extraordinarily cost-effective way of taking information to people. To me, as a community worker it is a wonderful example of people defining their own needs and making things happen at quite a low cost.

Lillian King As far as I know there is nothing else like this. Some people come along and say: 'Why isn't there one outside the Tilehurst Asda?' We say: 'We are not actually anything to do with Asda, although they let us park here', but it would be great if there were. Woodley would also be an ideal place to have one.

Initially it was called the Mobile Action Group because this is how this group of people saw themselves but we changed our name 18 months ago to Mobile Information Centre because we hoped the emphasis had shifted from action and lobbying for change in the community to information. The community has become more settled; it's not quite as mobile as it was. Because of the recession, families are staying and there are more children around.

Quite a lot of the work we do is referring the people to the appropriate agency, particularly a lot of people in this, dare I say it, affluent middle-class area who have been hit for the first time financially, don't know where to start, never had to claim benefits, wouldn't know how to go about it. We are a non-threatening organisation, and we can say: 'This is what's available for everyone, go and try.' We are independent, we are not judgmental, we are not going to report them to anybody, and we don't ask people's names or addresses. Everything is confidential and everything is free.

The difficulty about information is knowing what's available and knowing what to ask for. If we don't have it, we know a woman who does! Benefits are our biggest enquiry, and transport, under-fives provision, playgroups, leisure and more and more health concerns like free NHS dentists and carers.

We have people from all over the place. Two Americans straight from Heathrow were trying to get to Henley and were lost here. It's amazing how many people find themselves in this car park.

Mobile Information Centre *drawn by Shakila Mushtaq*

Once a chap came along with a bucket and said 'Is there a tap here? I want to wash my car.' I burst out laughing, I think he was rather offended. One lady had been sent by her husband with a list of things to ask us. Lots of children ask if we're selling ice-cream!

The caravan lives outside Earley Community Centre and gets towed back there – Eric, Jenny and Douglas do the towing. We have about 14 volunteers in the project. It is an invaluable commitment.

We have been offered the use of a room by Earley Town Council as a base but we don't want to shift our work over there. The idea of having a caravan is slightly novel. It is the business of not having to open the door and make any effort. In a way I would be sad to see a purpose-built community centre.

Gill Flanagan We are looking to develop the project, particularly for the disabled and for carers, and perhaps in other parts of Earley. This van will have to be retired but it wouldn't be put out to grass. There are other groups in the area who could use it. I shall be terribly sorry to see it go, but we are looking forward to moving on.

Montpellier House, Kings Road

Surveyor Cliff Campbell explains why he still thinks of Montpellier House, in Kings Road, as 'Rambo's Hideout', and local historian Tony Barham tries to shed a little light on its mysterious occupant.

Cliff Campbell About a year ago, my employers sent me with an assistant to take measurements in one of the old stone-faced houses in Kings Road, Reading, near the corner where it joins Orts Road.

I had nearly finished my work when I heard my colleague talking to some people by the front steps. After a time he came in looking puzzled and said that a Japanese family were outside asking if this was the house where Rambo lived.

Thinking this must be some kind of joke, I went out and found a very respectable-looking family consisting of father, mother and teenage daughter, who told us they came from Hiogo, in the island of Honshu. After some discussion I gathered that they were looking for the house where the poet Arthur Rimbaud had stayed, many years ago.

My colleague looked quite relieved. I think he had been expecting a desperate gunman to appear at any moment. As for the poet Rimbaud, we could not help them much. I suggested that they make some inquiries at Reading College of Technology nearby, and also gave them directions to the university.

My mate remains convinced that it was all a big CIA plot and still refers to the building, when we pass it, as 'Rambo's Hideout'.

Tony Barham The symbolist poet Arthur Rimbaud, who was associated with the poet Paul Verlaine, may have paid a brief visit to Reading in 1872, when he was 18. Some letters, formerly in the possession of Miss Blizzard, of the Collegiate School, indicate that he stayed in Kings Road for some months in 1874.

It seems likely that, for the greater part of his time in Reading, Rimbaud did not stay at Montpellier House, then occupied by M le Clair, a Professor of French, and his successors. He is more likely to have stayed a few doors away at the school run by Mr William Watson. It seems probable that he paid his way by teaching French for Mr Watson and perhaps also for M le Clair.

Letters written some years after the event by John Cuthbert of Reading, which cannot be treated as entirely reliable, refer to Rimbaud as 'the young Monsieur who knows the poet Verlaine'. We are told of an outing by train to Henley and then by horse-drawn barge to Medmenham, to view excavations and earthworks at Bolebec Castle.

Whether the trip included a visit to Medmenham Abbey is, unfortunately, left uncertain, for stories of the former disreputable society, known as 'The Monks of Medmenham', might have influenced the young Rimbaud's alleged interest in alchemy and occultism.

Local tradition tells that, at about the same period, the older lads of Mr Watson's school would sometimes resort to a small alehouse in Orts Road, called The Dove, and kept by a carpenter called Goodey. The place was officially out of bounds to the 'young gentlemen' but seems to have been used by both pupils and teachers until a later headmaster threatened to ask the Justices to have the place closed unless it ceased to serve anyone from the school.

If Rimbaud went there, it would be interesting to know what they thought of him. His reputation as a poet was insignificant at that time.

Rimbaud gave up poetry while he was still young and survived being shot by Verlaine, who was imprisoned for two years. At one stage in his life Rimbaud lived with a gang of tramps, searching for food in dustbins. He is said to have joined the Dutch Foreign Legion, deserting three weeks after arriving in Indonesia, and later worked as a seaman on a British ship. Eventually he settled in Harrar in Ethiopia where he is said to have been involved in gun-running and the slave trade.

A cartoon of Rimbaud by Verlaine

Museum of Reading

The most impressive aspect of the Museum, Art Gallery and Town Hall complex can be seen from the Friar Street end of Blagrave Street. When you turn back to look at the whole group of buildings, they make a particularly fine Victorian ensemble. In 1989 the museum moved out of its original rooms in the Town Hall as part of a complete refurbishment of the building. Four years later the first of the new galleries was opened in the Town Hall. The Principal Keeper of Collections, Leslie Cram, has worked there for nearly 20 years.

When I started here in September 1974 I was told: 'Whatever you do, although you are employed as an archæologist, you must never go out of the building. You must never dig.' This was because a separate excavation unit was being set up and I was there to administer it. My interest isn't so much in digging, because quite often you haven't the slightest idea of what you've dug up until later. You're covered in mud, it's four o'clock, it's raining and you can't go home and have your tea. My interest is with the objects and the story they tell. You can't assess what you've unearthed until you are back in the laboratory and examining it at your leisure.

One of the most exciting discoveries that we have in the museum was made in 1981/82 during the excavations at the Abbey Wharf where the new Abbey Gardens site was being developed. This is the area where the Holy Brook meets the Kennet. We have a stretch of mediæval timbers from that excavation on show in the New Gallery. There was great archæological interest in this development, the excavations are all recorded and analysed, and we are hoping to see it published soon.

Another significant discovery that I particularly treasure came about four years ago as the result of a phone call from the gravel pit at Caversham. They had turned something up and wanted me to go and see what it was. They showed me some huge timbers, scatterings of pottery, old agricultural implements and a particularly interesting decorated panel of lead.

Later that day, at about midnight, when I was trying to sleep but wondering what it could all possibly be, it suddenly dawned on me that it was the timbers of a Roman well. The excavating bucket had scooped up the whole of the base of a well with all sorts of odds and ends that had been thrown down it.

The excavation team at Oxford confirmed my conclusions and added that they were convinced that the lead was from a rare liturgical tank. Only 16 or so had been found previously and it was possibily connected with Christianity. The puzzle was, where was the Chi-Rho? The Chi-Rho is one of the symbols used by the early Christians, being the first letters in Greek for Christ. When the lead panel was delivered to the museum a few days later, I was the first person to recognise that Christian symbol on it since it had been put into the well in Roman times.

Reading Museum *photo by John Rogers*

The discovery was announced in the *Daily Telegraph* and *The Times* because of its interest to the whole nation.

It was an exciting discovery of the earliest Christianity in the area. The pottery from the well is about 350 AD which ties in with the date of a period of non-Christian uncertainty, after Christianity became the adopted religion of the Roman Empire in 310 AD. The symbol would have been incriminating evidence during this time when there could have been persecution, so the possible explanation is that the side of the lead tank with the Chi-Rho on was cut off and thrown down the well.

Leslie
Cram

I was also involved in arrangements to put concrete on top of the old Abbey wall instead of demolishing it to make way for the Inner Distribution Road round the Forbury. We wanted to leave the wall for future generations. We're like the Vatican here. We think in terms of 500 to 1,000 years ahead. Some time in the future, the Forbury IDR will be redeveloped and the archæologists then will know they can have a look at the Abbey wall underneath.

One interesting bit of the wall we did retrieve bore a carving of a head. My investigations into its history took me to Wells Cathedral, where there are similar carvings. We are sure it is the head of a bishop because it has a bishop's mitre and we interpret it as a saint who was a bishop specially connected with Reading. Possibly it is of Thomas Becket, the Archbishop who officially opened Reading Abbey in 1164, and who became a very important saint after he was murdered by order of King Henry II. I am pleased that the head is used for our museum poster.

❀ *Bouquet* **Town Hall**

The Town Hall is seriously beautiful, a wonderful piece of architecture with its mixture of styles – high Gothic, Romanesque, Victorian – a statement of civic pride and a monument to the history of trading in Reading.
Jon Everitt

Nellie Ward's Shop, Mount Pleasant

Nellie Ward was one of the great Reading characters. She ran Ward's Shop, which used to stand next to The Greyhound, in Mount Pleasant, before it became part of the extended pub. Nellie died in 1979 at the age of 90 but her name is still remembered at The Greyhound by the bar which is named after her.

Iris Millis, *from Langley, met Nellie in the 50s.* I have never met anyone like her, I loved her right away. She was larger than life, about 20 stone and quite short. Her straight dark hair was short, with a clip at the side to keep it tidy. She always wore a dark dress with a white apron to cover her, tied at the back with a bow. Her eyesight was very poor and she wore thick lenses. She went blind later on.

Nellie's Berkshire accent was wonderful to hear and I was spellbound by her tales of childhood in Reading – I called them Aunt Nell's tales She would sit in the next door garden with a slab of ice cream and wafers and while we were talking she would cut it up and eat the slices – they called them Berkshire Hogs. I can never remember ever laughing so much.

It was years earlier, in about 1927, when Nellie, her husband, and children Ivy, Bill, Daisy and Dick, took over the shop in Mount Pleasant. Ivy, and William 'Jerry' Taylor, her husband, recalled how it came about.

Ivy Taylor I was about 10 and we were living at No 6, next to the shop at No 8. It was called Neale's then and Miss Neale and her father lived there.

Jerry Taylor Miss Neale courted a chap name Blackhall when she was a girl and he went on some sort of expedition with dog sledges in Canada. They got lost in the snow and they all got killed except him. He was the only one that was found but he had lost all his fingers and toes with frostbite.

Ivy Miss Neale never ever met anyone else. She was quite old when he came back but she married him and moved to Castle Hill, in Maidenhead. That was when she offered the shop to mum and we moved next door and changed the name from Neale to Ward. It was a sweet shop then and later on we sold coal as well, and other things like fireworks and bundles of wood. In Blake's Lock Museum they've got the green scales my mum used to serve up the coal.

The other side of The Greyhound was a blacksmith's shop, belonging to Jack Scearce – we watched them shoeing the horses. Jack Scearce used to own the pub as well and when we lived at No 6 he'd to call over the railings to my dad on a Sunday morning, 'Give us your jug, Dick', and he'd fill it up with beer. The Scearces had a yard at the side and an Italian family, the Colangelos, who lived in Silver Street, used to keep their barrel organs there with their monkeys. Mr Colangelo would tune up the organs in the yard and us kids would ask if we could turn the handle. One day my brother was playing about with a monkey and it bit his ear and we had to rush him to the hospital.

My mum used to sell all sorts of things, like chitterlings. Me and my sister Daisy used to go round to Venners with a trolley and get two sets of chitterlings. We watched them kill the pigs and we had to wait for them to get the entrails out. I had the job of washing all the entrails out under the cold water tap, and mum used to soak them overnight. They used to come out as white as a sheet. They were lovely and we sold loads of them.

Then my mum made ice cream and me and my sister had the job of going down to the factory in Vastern Road, pushing an old truck, and getting two sacks of broken ice. It was cheaper than buying a block. Then we had to run all the way home from Vastern Road before it melted, and it was running through the bottom of the truck. The wheel kept coming off on the cobbles and I had to keep going into the leather shop on the way home and ask the man if he could come out and put a nail in my truck. Oh, we had some real fun in those days.

There were three lodging houses in Silver Street. One was called Mary Anne's – that was the name of the old lady who kept it – and all the tramps used to call in there for just a night's kip. Some of them would stay there for four or five weeks. My mum was such a good old soul they used to come up and say: 'Don't your dinners smell lovely, Mrs Ward, we haven't had a roast potato for ages.' And she'd say: 'Well, if you peel the potatoes and bring them up in a dish, I'll cook them for you.' She used to put in roast potatoes on a Sunday and we had dishes of them and the tramps used to come up and collect them. She was very jolly and ever so kind.

There were quite a few fights at the lodging-houses. We used to sleep up in the attic, me and my sister, and we'd take the old candle up there and 10 o'clock of the night, you could rely on it, especially weekends, you'd hear screaming, and we'd jump out of bed and shout down the attic stairs: 'Mum, there's a fight'. She'd get her coat on and so would we and my father would go mad. He used to say: 'Stay in, you're not letting those girls go', and they'd be fighting down there.

Nellie Ward

When we were in the shop, we all used to sit outside on summer nights. The summers really were summers then and used to go on right into September and the sky never ever seemed to get black. We used to sit out the front till about one in the morning and everybody would come out with their chairs and sit round the pavement. My friends had an old horn gramophone and they used to bring it out and we danced up and down the pavement at night. You'd have spring onions and nice crusty cottage loaves and cheese. It used to be really lovely. You could leave your doors and windows wide open and nobody would ever come in. I think we had the best times then.

My mother only rented the shop. St Giles's Church owned the pub and the two shops and they sold it to Simmons, the brewery, and as soon as Simmons got hold of it they wanted to get rid of the shop so they could extend The Greyhound. My mum went to live in Bartletts Cottages in Castle Street, then to Coley Flats, Wensley Road, and eventually with us in Mount Pleasant. She was in a home at the corner of Northumberland Avenue for the last four years and by the time she died she was totally blind.

Right up until she died, she would go to The Greyhound. When Mr Mowbray was there he used to have a band and they'd get out the cymbals and the drums and my old mum used to bang on the old drum and sing. She loved it. She was really a lively character she was, always ready for a laugh. They used to pull her leg at The Greyhound and they all loved her, even the young lads. Every weekend she'd say: 'Are we going down The Greyhound again?' Just after Mum died, Mr Mowbray asked me: 'Would you mind if we named the bar after your mum?' She would have been proud of that. I wish she could have lived long enough to see that.

New Testament Church of God, Caversham

The Rev Ahira Lawrence came to Reading in September 1983 from Coventry to take over the pastorship of the New Testament Church of God, in Caversham. The congregation used to worship at the Providence Chapel, in Oxford Road, before moving into its present home, the cream and brown building, next to Caversham Library on Church Street, which still resembles what it was in its previous life – the Glendale cinema.

Pastor Lawrence The church in Coventry was a regular old church so this building was quite different for me. At that time, we were not privileged to have many buildings for ourselves – we came into the country doing church work – so when we got a building we really appreciated the opportunity very much and thanked God for it, especially when it has a setting like this. I wasn't here when the building was bought but it was dedicated to the Lord and it became sacred ground. It was quite suitable for a church and didn't need much conversion. It still has a lot of the older things, like the balcony, and the projectionist's rooms, which are used by the Sunday school. Every part has its purpose. I had a new floor put in because the old one sloped down towards the screen. The screen was taken down, the wall at the back was plastered and two rostrums were built. The baptistry is actually under the rostrum where the preacher stands, so when we have baptisms we just lift the top off and there is the baptism pool.

The setting is good because this is in the centre of Caversham, not far from schools and stations. People come to worship here from all over Reading and it is a multi-cultural congregation. A lot of people believe it is a West Indian church, a black people's church, but it is just a black-led church; it is for everybody and all nationalities. It started in the United States, more than 100 years ago, and its headquarters are in Cleveland, Tennessee. It is known there as the Church of God but when it came to the West Indies there was a Church of God already so, in order to be registered, we had to call it New Testament Church of God. A lot of people thought we only dealt with the New Testament but that is not so.

There is a strong family feeling in the church, just as we have in the West Indies, a close-knit community. You should see this building at funeral services when the community turns out. We have the church filled to the balcony. If it is a well-known person, we are packed to capacity and about half again outside. That is our original custom. You don't have to be invited to a funeral, you just

New Testament Church of God *by Shakila Mushtaq*

go. For a Christian departure, we have a joyful time, mixed with sorrow; for a non-Christian it is a sadder occasion. There are two places after death, just like home and prison here on earth. God has the same order, Heaven and whatever you want to call it, Hades or Hell, but it is a place where happiness is not.

We grew rapidly when I first came here, then it slowed down like all churches. True born-again Christian churches grow slower than others because there is a lot of commitment to Christianity, it is a bigger step to take. You are changing from one life to another.

I like it here in Reading but I feel like I want a change. Pastors in our church go wherever they send us. We are allotted to a circuit for four years and then they can ask us to move on again to another church. I can ask for a transfer if I want to go but generally they do the changing and we go where we are needed most.

There is a General Assembly every two years where all the churches, nationally and internationally, meet in the US, and make decisions on doctrine and practical matters and choose the overseers. This year we have a change of overseer here in England. The new overseer was at the Brixton Church and, when he takes over, somebody has to be sent to Brixton. So who knows…!

I oversee a big area – Reading, Aylesbury, Oxford, and High Wycombe. People tell me I seem to be preaching more than ever. Sometimes I feel I want to go home to the Lord, but then I think, 'I don't want to die now because I have a lot of preaching to do.' There are no forces of the devil to fight against in Heaven.

Progress Theatre, The Mount

The Progress Theatre was founded in 1946, but it did not find its permanent home for five years. Plays were performed in Palmer Hall, West Street, but members had to hold rehearsals, paint scenery and store props where they could. At last they found the Mildmay Hall, in The Mount, which was transformed into a theatre by members and friends. The first production to be held there was Sheppey, *by Somerset Maugham, which opened in October 1951.*

Pat Tyler, an active member of the theatre for more than 40 years, wrote about the theatre's history before her death in 1993:

The Mildmay Hall has an interesting history for the site was purchased over 100 years ago by Mr Martin Hope Sutton of Sutton's Seeds. He also bought the Pheasant Inn (where Mildmay Cottage now stands) and the licence of the inn. On part of the site he erected a small hall and founded a working men's club to be used for billiards, darts and various other games. There was a small library and refreshments were served – not liquor, of course, as the Suttons were a teetotal family.

During the First World War, a brick wing, consisting of two rooms, was added to the building and the hall was used as an extension to Sutherlands, a house used as a hospital by the Berkshire branch of the British Red Cross Society. Between the two World Wars the building was used for various purposes including a boys' club. At the beginning of the Second World War, 16 evacuee children from the East End of London were accommodated there for a short while and later the WVS used it as a store for large quantities of clothes. The building was sold in 1949 to the Reading Co-operative Society who rented it to Progress for £50 a year.

In 1964, after a mammoth fund-raising effort, Progress bought the theatre for £3,000 – the Co-op had generously offered it at the original 1949 purchase price. The theatre now has about 150 paid-up members and 270 Friends or patrons and life members. It has a busy programme and each year presents six or seven main productions, which run for nine or ten nights, four or five short runs and numerous one or two-night productions. Dorothy Grugeon, who was original-ly a member of the Progress Student Group, is currently the theatre secretary and she recollects some memorable occasions in the life of the theatre.

To be secretary of the Progress Theatre is, I feel, an honour and a responsibility: we have a very high standard and a long-standing reputation to maintain. My predecessor was Pauline Gray, an ex-professional who joined Progress some 20 years ago. She and her husband, Harry, are both leading actors with us. Pauline is now a Trustee and Harry is also an experienced director. They were both particularly helpful to Kenneth Branagh when, as a member of the Progress Student Group, he decided that he would like to try for entry to RADA. It is nice to know that Ken has never forgotten Progress Theatre. He has been extremely supportive over the last four or five years helping us, by his presence, to raise money towards the theatre building fund.

Progress Theatre *drawn by Shakila Mushtaq*

Dorothy
Grugeon

The theatre is totally self-funding. It is quite miraculous as each year goes by when we look at our balance sheet that we are still there, because essentially what we now have is a small business run by part-time people. Everything is done in whatever time any of us have to give and I think we should be quite proud of ourselves that we have managed to continue on that basis.

We'd got to the point in about 1988 where the premises really were too small. We had to move forward and build additional rooms. After several quotations, we ended up with one which was going to be about £35,000. Until that point, we had not even had a bank loan, but it occurred to one or two of us that we occupy the best part of an acre of land in what is now a conservation area, and that the land itself must be worth a fair amount of money. The bank agreed to give us a 10-year mortgage facility but in order to keep the repayments as low as possible we had to fund-raise.

Pauline Gray contacted Ken Branagh and asked if there was any way he could help. Without any hesitation, he said yes, he would speak to the Hexagon Theatre and arrange with them a charity preview of his Hollywood film, *Dead Again*, and all the proceeds, every penny of them, had to go to Progress Theatre. I was the publicity officer then so I was the main connection between his film distributors at their London offices, Ken's office and the Hexagon. I was juggling names and publicity in a way I'd never done before. This was a whole new scenario to me, dealing with film companies, and the secrecy involved, all very exciting.

As the director of the film, Ken insisted we had to keep it secret from any other cinema that we were getting this preview. It went ahead in September 1991 and he said he would come down and attend it. We filled the Hexagon to overflowing with no problem at all. The sum total from that one performance was nearly £6,000, which helped our fund enormously. Ken's generous gesture was much appreciated.

We still have a very strong Student Group, founded soon after Progress started. I like to think that we are helping young people, via the group, to develop an interest in the arts as well as giving them self-confidence generally. It seems that sport is always funded, but not everyone is sports minded nor capable of participating in them. It is a pity that the arts are not funded to the same extent, because they are just as important to everyone's quality of life.

Reading Abbey

One of the great religious communities of mediæval Britain, Reading Abbey was founded in 1121 by William the Conqueror's son, Henry I, supposedly out of grief at the drowning of his son, and completed 200 years later in 1314. One of the richest Benedictine monasteries in England, the Abbey was the seat of Parliament on various occasions, was the scene of John of Gaunt's marriage to Blanche of Lancaster, and was used as an occasional residence by King Henry VIII. Four centuries of dominance ended with the dissolution of the Abbey in 1539 and its destruction over the years. Only the ruins remain today. Roisin O'Callaghan reflects on what the Abbey means to her and what significance it can still have to Reading in the 21st century.

In a quiet, restful, almost-forgotten part of the town are the open, roofless remains of the once proud Abbey of Reading. Conceived through the sorrow of a King, it was to experience a rich and varied history during its 400 years as the third most important abbey in the country.

Roisin O'Callaghan

When skilled workmen arrived with the first abbot to build the abbey, no one could have envisaged how they would be the forerunners of the diverse demands of a modern industrial town. Not only did they provide the foundations for industry but they must have contributed to the developing trade. History tells us that all was not well between the town's guilds and the abbey as the burghers increasingly struggled for independence. Men still struggle to improve their working conditions.

The abbey's influence was all-pervasive in all areas of life, caring for the sick, beggars and even furnishing means of entertainment – a plaque shows that the song, *Summer is a cumin' in*, was written here. It also lent itself to royal and state occasions. When I look at those solid flintstone walls open to all the elements, I see them as a tribute to the full range of human emotions, ambitions, achievements and aspirations. Now just the gaunt walls remain.

But its openness also symbolises the birth of a thriving town with all its complications reflected in the history of the abbey. The influence of this heritage, raised in the glory of God, which even the dissolution could not completely destroy, has spread onwards toward the 21st century. Let us treasure our proud heritage.

Reading Girls' School, Northumberland Avenue

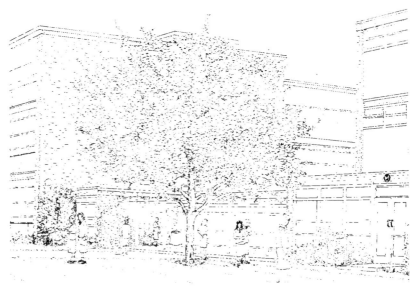

Reading Girls' School *drawn by Clive Hacker*

Reading Girls' School started its life as Southlands School, built on land which was formerly used by a pig farm and allotments. It was the fourth of the new secondary schools to be built at that time by the Reading Education Committee as part of its development plan. It was opened in 1960 and the girls from George Palmer Secondary School, which had outgrown its old building, moved in at the beginning of the summer term.

Dot Parish was living opposite the school site in the days when it was still allotments, one of them owned by her father-in-law. 'Hexham Road wasn't built then, there was just a wide open space,' she recalls. 'There were still pigs around the edges of the playground when the school was opened.' And June Gray, who has been the school caretaker for 15 years, can remember girls feeding the pigs at lunchtime.

Dot Parish saw Southlands being built. 'The builders were just finishing off the gym when the roof collapsed. After the roof was rebuilt, the builders had to come back because the copper they used interfered with our televisions.' That wasn't the end of the troubles as June Gray remembers. 'A year after the school opened the gym wall fell down and just when you thought nothing more could go wrong, a science room burnt down. But that was really all that happened apart from a few floods!'

The school was designed to accommodate 680 girls and was full from the start. Barbara Clifford, who was a new girl in September 1961, recalls how big it seemed. 'So many people went there that some of the classes had more than 40 pupils.

Dot Parish

'On my first day at Southlands I was told to go to the main hall. Our names were called out and we had to go to a particular group – all the classes were streamed, with the G-stream for the most intelligent girls, who were expected to go to college or university. The teacher I was supposed to have called us out but I didn't hear and went with the wrong group of girls – the G-stream. I had been in this group for half an hour before I was collected and taken to my class, upper A.'

Southlands was what is now considered a typical, functional sixties building, with its steel frame, brick walls, concrete floors and timber cladding. Dot Parish, who has lived opposite the school for 34 years, thinks the front of the building is 'beautiful'. To Barbara, as a young school girl, it was the height of modernity. 'I thought it was wonderful, particularly the lecture hall. It was a real treat to go in there.'

The modern facilities also impressed Miss Norma Crockett who arrived at Southlands at the same time as Barbara, but as a teacher of PE. 'My first impressions were that it seemed huge,' she said. 'The corridors seemed extremely long and it was easy to get lost.' She remembers there were teething problems in those early days with regular electrical gremlins. 'Welsh slate was used to decorate and border some of the windows, but these were liable to fall and could have caused a bad accident, so they were replaced by plastic.'

In the 70s, the number of girls soared to nearly 900 and the school had to expand. Miss Crockett remembers the Art and Music block, the Sixth Form area, the Modern Languages area, an extra Science room, a Careers room, and a new dining room all being added in 1975.

Miss Crockett retired in 1993 after more than 30 years at the school, teaching first PE, then Geography and Humanities. She still comes in to do some supply teaching and has retained her affection for the school. 'I like the friendly atmosphere, the brickwork which looks like new, the soft grey colour of the gym, the little courtyard next to the staffroom, and the cherry trees in front of the school,' she said. 'The place has

Norma
Crockett

become part of me and I have grown to respect the people who live in the area.'

Many of the teachers left a lasting impression on the girls. The first headmistress, Miss Hutchinson, was nicknamed 'Hutch' by the girls and Barbara Clifford said that 'if you saw her coming down the corridor you would quake in your boots. Everyone respected her.'

Tiena Elliott, who was at the school from 1965 until 1970, said: 'There were no male teachers then.' She and Barbara vividly remembered the English teacher who arrived at school in plain clothes with a head scarf and then appeared in class transformed with make-up, smart suits and matching, high stiletto shoes. Then, when she went home, she would change into her plain clothes again.

The girls themselves wore navy blue uniforms, with gold girdles and gold ties. Paula Priest, who started at the school in 1976, said: 'We pulled threads in our ties so that black stripes appeared. I wonder if that's where they got the idea for the stripes they have on the ties now.'

The girls all wore berets or hats and pleated skirts were forbidden. There was a constant battle over skirt lengths, particularly when the mini was popular. Shoes were black with no heels, long hair had to be tied back, and chewing gum was strictly forbidden.

Barbara and Tiena liked being in a new and modern building 'with lots of wood and impressionist pictures hanging on the wall', but Paula and Debbie Hawkins, who were at the school in the 70s, remember plain walls, painted in cream or magnolia. 'I loved the art room and spent time in there,' said Debbie, who admits playing truant sometimes. 'I used to hate needlework though. I made a pinafore dress but it went wrong so I cut it up and chucked it out of the window.'

Paula thought the rules were strict. 'We weren't allowed to go behind any buildings, or wear any make up or jewellery. There were a lot of fights and a few of my friends got the ruler or slipper.'

In the early years, the waiting area for visitors used to double as the canteen so if visitors came at lunch time they were surrounded by pupils. School meals were served on trolleys, Barbara remembers, with a bowl of vegetables in the middle of the tables. 'The food used to be fill-you-up type of stuff but if it was Gypsy Tart day people used to go mad!'

Nowadays dinner controllers like Mrs Cartwright and Mrs Barnes look after the girls at lunchtimes. Their main grumble is the school has too many doors, which makes it difficult to keep the girls out during lunch periods.

The school of the 90s is a different place from Southlands School, built on open land and 'miles from the trolley buses'. It is in the heart of residential Reading, surrounded by houses, and is prone to vandalism like most schools today. A new herb garden and pond supply a patch of green in the bricks and concrete – the school is highly environmentally conscious. It is much more open to the community now and is used in the

June Gray

evenings, weekends and holidays. There is a dancing school on Sundays, a rock and roll evening on Fridays, keep fit classes and car boot sales.

It became grant maintained in 1990 and acquired its new name, Reading Girls', in 1993 as part of the process of raising standards and building images. There are about 400 girls attending now but numbers are growing again. 'It's so much better now than it used to be in so many ways,' said June Gray, whose three girls all went to the school. She notices changes in the pupils as well as the building. 'They are more mature than they used to be, so it's not only that the school is much better but the pupils are better now.'

Barbara and Tiena, looking over their old school, agreed it is 'brilliant'. 'I wish I was here now instead of then,' said Tiena.

❀ *Bouquet* Science laboratory, Reading Girls' School

It is beautiful in here. The desks are made of a material that looks like marble. They are shaped as hexagons and have no rough edges. This room has a DIY smell, it is a clean smell. The walls are peach and the floor is pink. It is a bright and cheerful room. Everything goes together except for the odd blinds and windows. The sinks are white, and nice and new. They aren't blocked up. This room makes me feel like I want to work. When I look out of the window I can see the green field that slopes upwards. I can see rows of houses, the tennis court and lots of trees. It gives me a feel of life and freedom.

Rachel Grigg, 9R

Reading Remand Centre

When Reading Gaol was completed in 1844, the Illustrated London News *described the new building as 'from every side the most conspicuous building and, architecturally, by far the greatest ornament to the town'. The imposing county gaol, close to the Abbey site, was built of red Tilehurst bricks, enclosed by an 18ft boundary wall with a turret on each corner. It remained unchanged until the 1970s when there was a major modernisation programme which added a modern two-storey industrial block and swept away outbuildings, the turrets and the main gateway.*

The prison has had a varied career. During the First World War, it became HM Place of Internment for 'enemy' aliens, and then stood empty for 20 years. The Canadian Army used it as a military detention prison during World War Two, after which it was taken over for Corrective Training. From 1951 to 1969 it was a Borstal institution, then, experimentally, housed 'Rule 43' prisoners who were at risk from fellow inmates. The prison reverted to its old use as local gaol for the Thames Valley area in 1978 until the spring of 1992, when it became HM Remand Centre, Reading, for young male offenders aged between 17 and 21.

Reading Gaol's most famous prisoner, Oscar Wilde, was incarcerated there from November 13 1895 to May 18 1897. He immortalised the prison in The Ballad of Reading Gaol, *dedicated to the memory of Charles Thomas Wooldridge, a Trooper in the Royal Horse Guards, who was hanged at the prison on July 7 1896 for the murder of his wife. Nearly 100 years later, two young inmates wrote about their impressions of the prison.*

First inmate The main building is a monstrous mixture of concrete, metal and sharp angles. The history goes back to Victorian times, 1844, when the architects took the Gothic look and used it with pride, with its sturdy structure and threatening looks. They built their buildings to last. Personally I think it's got a dark and sad appearance. I think they purposely built it this way, to put inmates in a depressed state, but I do not, will not, let this affect me because if I do I would constantly be feeling aggrieved, thinking of my friends and family back in Stevenage and wondering how long we will be parted. Although I have strong feelings about being here, I refuse to take notice.

Reading Remand Centre *drawn by an inmate*

The building has a weird feeling to it that is kind of creepy. I don't know if it's to do with the building's age or the fact that, when the prison first opened, inmates were hanged to death where the exercise yard is today. Whatever it is, I get the feeling of the inmates being in a depressed state when I look at the exterior of the building. But, truth to tell, the inmates are, as a whole, happy and without worry. Maybe the Government chose to keep this monstrous part of English history as a prison, keeping us away from society because of its appearance, cold and unfeeling.

The new building is a spring chicken compared to the Victorian building. It's horrendously too modern a building for its Victorian counterpart. Built in the late 1970s, it looks like the back of a sports centre or a swimming pool. It is also a mix of concrete, metal and sharp angles. I think it looks like a disastrous attempt at a modern form of the Gothic look, and the effect of old and new together leaves the whole prison looking comically ugly.

Second inmate The remand centre is a grotesque building with a big wall around the outside and bars at the windows. It is a very old building and it seems that there could be ghosts in here because there was a lot of capital punishment back in the olden days. There were gallows in the exercise yard where many got hanged. It was known as Reading Gaol. To think I am in a building where people were in death row. It puts the shivers down my spine.

It used to be a Borstal and it was very strict. The chance of people coming back to the Borstal was 20 per cent but it is something like 80 per cent now. So what is wrong with today's punishment? Is it too soft? The first time I was sent to prison I had a knot in my stomach, I was really frightened. But the moment I was in there I was all right. It's that moment when the gate shut – I jumped out of my skin. I thought: that is the end of my freedom.

A lot of people have tried to commit suicide. You can understand why, doors being slammed behind you constantly and you are always thinking of the outside. The prison is a terrible looking place on the inside. It has steel doors and people holding keys and with suits like the police wear and big gates. The education block is the only place that doesn't look like a prison. It's like a school on the inside and on the outside it looks like any other part of the prison but it is the only place you can feel free.

❀ *Bouquet* **Prudential Building**

One of Reading's major employers takes over the derelict site of one of the town's founding industries to build its new national headquarters. Is it a worthy successor? I think so. An eye-catching, distinctive and generally symmetrical (without being mirrored) design immediately attracts interest and attention to the building. The inherent harshness of modern structural materials and construction methods are tempered by the use of natural stone facing materials and pleasing brickwork, resulting in a colour scheme that appears warm and welcoming.

Viewed from across the river (with the new footbridge making the island garden accessible) into the central courtyard with its ornamental garden, this is a building of which both the Prudential and Reading can be proud. See it floodlit at night!
Neal Marsden

The Rising Sun Institute, Silver Street

Where could the pimps, prostitutes and honest poor of Reading's 19th century slums go when they were not 'working'? The Rising Sun Institute opened in 1877 as a Temperance Institute, offering an alternative to pubs to this underclass, and to the honest poor as well! It provided people with a place in which to meet, discuss books, attend evening classes, including a gym and drawing classes, and Bible classes on Sundays. There was also a soup kitchen and a library, and tea and coffee were available from 5am to 10pm.

After many years as a Temperance Institute, the building eventually became Cook's Farms and Garden Supplies when this had to relocate from the High Street in the 1940s. Over the years, local farming dwindled, and the demand for Cook's products dwindled to match.

When Cook's closed in 1987, the building was sold for redevelopment as office space but the recession, with its slump in property prices, put paid to that plan. The building stood empty for some three years. During this period of disuse, it once again attracted the vandals and thieves of the area – but in a much less positive way. They wrecked it, and stole every bit of lead pipe from the plumbing system to sell for scrap, and even took the knobs off the doors. In addition, standing empty and unheated encouraged the action of rot and decay.

In November 1990 a rescue party appeared. A few of the artists and musicians who had squatted the old Huntley and Palmer building moved in. They saw this as a chance to build their dream of an arts and community centre, and started putting the Rising Sun Institute to rights.

'There were holes in the floor, holes in the walls and holes in the ceiling,' said Danuta Derczynska, one of the volunteers.

After six days, the owner turned up with a squad of builders to throw them out. 'He and his men removed everything we'd brought into the building and put it on the street,' said volunteer Simon Chatterton. 'Then he discussed matters with us and agreed to let us store our stuff in the derelict cottages next door. In the middle of this discussion with the landlord, someone came round to try to buy some compost from us.

'Three days later we got a phone call from the landlord asking whether we'd like to rent the building for six months at £10 a month. We were flabbergasted, gobsmacked!

'What had impressed him was that during the six days we'd been in the building we'd managed to put all the floorboards down, fix up all the holes in the windows, reconnect the plumbing through the whole building, sort out the dodgy wiring and get the electricity back on.'

A team of volunteers set out to acquire the skills necessary to restore the building. Working capital consisted of a loan of £120 from a well-wisher, which was needed for plumbing fittings. Some months later, after a cold but rewarding labour, the volunteers, who had now learned to do plumbing and 'electrics' and painting, were ready to open up the refurbished arts and community centre to the public. The grand opening took place on February 8 1991.

'We worked on the building day and night until we could open it up for events,' said Simon. Carpets and curtains and furniture were nearly all rescued from local skips – including 12 sets of full-length curtains. Almost the only things that had to be bought were the plumbing fittings.

'Even though it was winter, we used to open the back door to let the warmth in,' said Simon. 'This building has a phenomenal capacity to retain cold. When we first opened, Sunday nights were film and veggie supper nights. I remember we used to hand out blankets to everybody who came to see the films. Everyone huddled around wrapped in thick duvets and blankets.'

People recognise The Rising Sun by the giant bas-relief sun on the north wall. 'Martin Hayward Harris created the plaque for a window display for Artworker, and then donated it to The Rising Sun,' said Danuta. 'He had to work on it to make it waterproof. When we put it up, one of the neighbours complained to the council. They told him that they had just registered it as a Public Work of Art.'

Today, The Rising Sun is flourishing under the direction of a core of volunteers that is still composed largely of the original group. Unlike the early days, they receive some council funding, and have even attracted some commercial sponsorship. With this help, and thousands of hours of voluntary work, the facilities of the centre have expanded.

'It's not like other arts centres because it gives a lot of people the chance to acquire new skills, especially local unemployed people who come here and give their services to the centre,' said volunteer Felix Brünner. 'It gives them something to do and builds up their self-esteem.'

The centre now boasts silk screen printing studios, art galleries, Reading's only vegetarian café, Reading's only venue for regular

The Rising Sun Institute *drawn by Tahaira Khan*

jazz/impro sessions, Reading's only venue for regular acoustic and roots music performances. In addition, it provides space and publicity for a host of community activities run by other groups – Thin Raft poetry readings, the Bubble and Squeak Club, Gherkins Comedy Club – and supports workshops from haiku poetry to Raku pottery.

'We want to keep expanding the range of activities,' said Simon. 'We would also love to have another building nearer the centre of Reading that would allow us a bigger venue.'

Royal Berkshire Hospital

The Royal Berkshire Hospital, in London Road, with its elegant frontage, is one of the most familiar landmarks in Reading. Opened on 27 May 1839, the hospital was designed by a local architect Henry Briant and built by public subscription on land donated by a former Prime Minister, Lord Sidmouth. There can be few Reading people more intimately linked with the hospital than John Evans, from Calcot. John, who has been registered blind for 10 years, was born there, worked there for 18 years, and has been attending the hospital's Medical Eye Centre as a patient all his life.

I was born in Benyon Ward, in the Royal Berks Hospital, on 22 October 1949. I've been going to the hospital as a patient since I was very young and I suppose my first recollections would have been when I was four or five because there was a rocking horse in the waiting room which I rode on. There was always the same smell, a sort of disinfectant smell, and the floors were very polished.

I wasn't frightened going there as a child. Mr Durrell, the surgeon, always reminded me of a father figure, he was very good to me. I used to go to the orthoptic department about once a year till I was 15 and then, unfortunately, I had a road accident and I now have to go back regularly. Through that accident I decided I wanted to work at the hospital.

I started working there in September 1971 and stayed for 18 years. I was laundry porter and my job was to take the laundry round on a hand trolley to all the wards and departments from the Eye Block, which was built in the 1960s, to the Nuffield block which was built just before the last war by Lord Nuffield.

Not many people know what my surname is – everyone thinks it's Laundry! It was a standing joke. The ward sisters would phone me and I'd say: 'Yes, this is John Laundry here.'

We reckoned we walked 13 miles a day round the hospital. It's all corridors, and all the wards and departments reminded me of little houses. All the wards had different atmospheres and a lot depended on the sisters in charge. I used to love the children's ward. Quite often, if I had an empty trolley, the kids would say, 'Can we have a ride?' so I would give them a ride to the door.

I had to go upstairs by lift, very old-fashioned, with trellis gates – that's now gone. Trolleys and even the patients went up in that old lift.

Royal Berkshire Hospital *drawn by Shakila Mushtaq*

Then there was the life of the other part of the hospital, the part people didn't see much, like the kitchens. On a Friday, if I got down there at about 12 o'clock, I regularly got a plate of fish and chips, but I had to hide in the cupboard, and in the afternoons I'd always go down to the stores for a cup of tea and a chat with Eric and the lads. You had the dining room and all the other departments down there – it was a little town on its own. Although I was visually impaired, I knew it like the back of my hand. I could still go there today and tell you where most of the places were.

Just toward the end, I left the laundry and went into the gardening department for a couple of years doing the repairs on the machinery. I still miss the camaraderie. I go to the hospital as a patient and I suppose I shall have to go there for the rest of my life. It's like going home. People still recognise you, that's the amazing part.

I always worked over Christmas, it was brilliant. We used to hurry up and go around the wards because we'd be invited to all the parties that were going on. I shall never forget my first party. Every ward I was going on they were saying, 'Come on, have a sherry with us', and I didn't

John
Evans

know how to handle it. When I got out of there I wasn't walking in a straight line!

At Christmas they always used to put on a sort of comedy and one I remember was called *Wind in the Pillows*. It took the Michael out of everybody, like one surgeon who was nicknamed the 'bran man' because all of his patients, no matter whether they were six months old or 90, were automatically put on to bran.

Then there was another guy, a former patient who got rushed in one Christmas just as all the festivities were starting. They saved his life, and he used to come back every Christmas, as regular as you'd set your clock, and he'd fish out the various staff he knew.

One Christmas some bright spark came up with the idea of a cycle ride to raise some money for some special equipment in the ICU. Me being me I said, 'If everybody else is willing, I am.' So anyway, 20 or 30 of us decided we would go on all sorts of bicycles. I made everyone laugh with this tiny little bicycle with a bag on the back containing a stove and kettle ready for a brew-up on the way home. I think we raised a couple of thousand pounds. That was the Berks. Everybody cared about everybody else.

People worked there for a very long time. To me it's just like a big family. I felt very privileged to work there, especially during a time when the health service was the health service. Come to think about it, I was born in 1949 when the health service started. I'll fight to make sure it stays.

◻ *Brickbat* **Queens House**

I think Queens House (the 'Metal Box' building) is a good candidate for 'most hideous building in Reading'. Positioned right next to the railway station where all visitors to Reading can see it, it is a huge lump of grey concrete. The building is circular with a hole in the middle. I worked there for a while for Digital and every floor was laid out the same. It was quite a challenge to find your own desk each day but visitors had no chance, they were forever wandering around lost.
Elaine Carthy

St Andrew's House, Wilton Road

St Andrew's House, in Wilton Road, has been through several name changes. Formerly known as Elm Lodge, it became St Andrew's Home at the turn of the century, then Wilton House, and has now reverted to St Andrew's. Described as a 'substantially erected residence called Elm Lodge', with pleasure gardens, grounds, an 18-acre park, and a farm of about 58 acres, it was auctioned on August 29 1867. Only 21 years later, when the property was auctioned again, it is mentioned as having frontages of several roads, indicating how quickly the area was being developed.

In 1902 Elm Lodge became St Andrew's Home, established by the Church of England Waifs and Strays Society, offering a home to 39 orphaned or homeless boys up to the age of 14, who attended local schools. By the Second World War, the number had risen to 50 residential boys but ideas in child care changed and the home was closed in 1962. It was bought by the James Butcher Housing Association in the 1970s and they built Marsh Court, a three-storey block of flats, at the back of the mansion. In 1978 they started restoring the house.

Peter Dent, *of the Housing Association* When we were renovating it, we were conscious of the fact that this is a listed building. The middle part of the building is Georgian and the semi-circular wings at either end were put in by the Victorians. Two front columns of the house had split from top to bottom, so the Civic Society, the Georgian Society, and Reading building inspectors all got involved.

In the end we replaced those columns with natural Bath stone, the same place the original stone came from but not the same pit. Each column cost £5,000.

Now restored, the house is occupied by the Association, Age Concern and Paramount Housing, and is very different from the days when Bill Cam lived there as one of the old 'home' boys. He came to St Andrew's in 1941, when he was only seven, and left when he was 14. He returned to the house for the first time in 46 years and talked about his feelings when he saw it.

Bill Cam The outside is unchanged so it felt as though I was going home. Walking through the door felt the same, but there was one thing missing, there was no noise of children running round. To me it was like a morgue. When it was a boys' home the corridor was out of bounds at certain times, so during the forbidden period, should

Bill Cam

any of the boys be there they were punished by the house-master or matron. Needless to say one day I happened to be out of bounds at the wrong time. It was then that I hid under the stair, whose creaking sound is indelibly printed in my mind as though it happened yesterday.

I was pleased to see the kitchen, the scullery and the cellar were exactly the same. The biggest disappointment was the disappearance of the gymnasium, and the beautiful grounds and orchard. The memories of long hours spent there were so vivid, sometimes playing, sometimes in punishment, under the gardener's watchful eye.

I remember how having to clean the scullery over and over again lost me the chance to participate in Reading School football trials. Despite getting up at 5am to start my work so that I could finish in time to get to the football ground, the headmaster, after several inspections, decided it was not good enough and ordered me to start all over again.

It was wartime, so I remember air raids, and sleeping downstairs. Raids were greatly welcomed because of the special treats we had. Cakes and jam came out on such occasions. Rules during the air raids were strict and clear, although I cannot remember how many minutes we had to get to the cellar before we were punished for being too slow. This meant our army-style kit bags were strategically placed for quick exits.

During one particular raid, I was halfway down the stairs to the cellar when I realised my friend Tom was not behind me. I went back and frantically shook him. Tom hardly stirred. In desperation I whacked him one on the head with my kit bag but the weight of the shoes at the bottom of the bag rendered him unconscious. I quickly raised the alarm and Tom was carried to safety. I was praised for being a good and brave boy for reporting Tom's difficulty!

We were fed and clothed well, thanks to the Church of England Society and the Red Cross. In fact we had so much food and fuel that some of us pinched coal and supplied our friends outside the home. Friday nights were bath nights, young ones first, and Saturday was Epsom salts day!

Religion played a big part in our home life. We had our own chapel and we had to go to church at least twice a day, sometimes

St Andrew's House *photo by John Rogers*

four times for older boys. There was hardly any manual work done on Sunday except for bare necessities. That was the only time we were allowed to play, from Saturday night, after we had done all our duties. Each boy, according to age, was given duties like looking after one or more young boys, including darning their socks. Like true brothers, we fought every day, but we were also loyal to each other. No outside boy dared touch one of the home boys. We were often picked upon because we had to wear a uniform. Even our Sunday best suits were all the same, grey. This automatically set us apart especially as we had to march to school. The local boys would watch us come and shout: 'The home kids are coming.' They would brace themselves at the gate in order to prevent us entering the school grounds. Here ended our neat and tidy clothing. They would try and keep us out of school. Once in, they attempted to keep us in the grounds so that we were constantly on the warpath and won most skirmishes.

The Guardians taught us to be individuals in our own right but working for the common good of the group and community. They drummed into us that we must respect women. All in all, they taught us a lot that was good for us although we neither knew nor liked it at the time. But I regret that family relationships were not addressed, like cousins, and aunts. I have had trouble working out who's who in that respect.

Although there were times when I thought I would never get out of that place, I did finally leave the home in 1948.

Yield Hall Car Park

I had come to think of London Street, once the prime 'character street' of Reading, as nowadays being scarcely worth a second glance. But that was until one clear, fine day in the early autumn of 1993, when, at 1.15pm, I was walking into the town by the east pavement and had almost reached the Reading Business Centre. Looking towards the heart of the town, I was stopped in my tracks by a sight I had never seen before and which I promptly christened the Fuscous Fingers Phenomenon; then I darted into a nearby office and invited a couple of the staff I knew to witness this strange event also.

Some months later, I saw, in that same spot, something else unusual in the nature of building-related phenomena, which I named the Phantom Gable Effect.

Both of these sights are to be observed over the top level of the Yield Hall Car Park in the correct conditions, but it seems to me that clear, sunny weather combined with very good visibility are necessary.

In the case of the Fuscous Fingers, what you see are great rays — smoky, not bright — fanning upward to the heavens from the town's rooftop horizon. And unlike the Phantom Gables, which require some seconds of training the eye upon any one of the gables of that car park parapet before the effect appears, the rays are noticed at once. The 'phantom' gable appears just a little above the true gable and is rather less distinct.

Clearly, in the case of the gables, it is the parapet, with its row of inverted v-shapes, which gives rise to the effect; but I cannot be quite sure yet whether the building is also responsible for those strange dark rays.

Bernard Redway

The Spinney, Earley

The Spinney *drawn by Tammy Dodsworth*

In the middle of what is claimed to be the largest housing estate in Europe, incongruously surrounded by modern executive homes, stands The Spinney, a 17th century thatched cottage with black beams and a well in the garden. Originally two farm cottages, it has been extended twice since the war, and until the 1980s was in the middle of farmland, owned by the Colebooks, who were Reading butchers.

Peter Colebrook, who sold the business nearly 20 years ago, moved into The Spinney in 1946. In 1964 the University of Reading bought the house and it became the home of the vice-chancellor Sir Harry Pitt. After the massive expansion of Lower Earley housing estate, The Spinney was acquired in 1990 by Jenny and Brian Cuff, who live there with their six-year-old son James.

Peter Colebrook My father bought the house early in the war. I had married in 1939 and we had never had a house of our own because I was away in the war, so my father thought it would be ideal for us when I got back. I knew the house, of course, because we owned the farmland all round it. The previous owners were the Allsebrooks, who made water pumps in Reading, and then a builder called Goodall. My father let the Goodalls go on living there during the war but fortunately they wanted to move away anyway so when I was demobbed we were able to move in. We were very lucky to have a house like that.

We never knew for certain how old it was. One person who came to look at the house said there were signs of cow manure in the walls, which they used in the 1600s. We built another wing with an extra bedroom and bathroom when we moved in, and our two children were born there. It looked quite normal then, a country cottage in an acre and a half of garden with farmland around. We had cattle there but it was too near Reading to keep sheep.

We moved out in 1964 for one reason only – the university wanted to buy our land. They built a new hall of residence there and the vice-chancellor Sir Harry Pitt lived in the cottage. I got planning permission to build a new house, Hillside House, which is now part of the Earley estate. We decided that as we had lived in a very old house, the new one would be ultra-modern.

Jenny Cuff We came from the centre of Reading and we had wanted something in the country but when we looked in the country all of a sudden the isolation came to the top of the agenda. Then we were given details of this house and we drove up and down the lane and said: 'They've got the details wrong; they've got the directions wrong. There's no such place.'

Finally I said, 'Right, you drive and I'll look,' and we flashed past the end of the drive and I saw the thatch and the black and white. 'It's true, there is such a house.' I could hardly believe it. As we came up the drive that January, we discovered this pearl in an ocean. It was like Alice in Wonderland. To this day that remains very much part of my feelings for the place. It's a beautiful house but there is this added element of magic.

When we looked at it, it was just like that – it was ours. We were the right people at the right time, everything appealed. It was magical.

Two years ago the thatch was renewed. The 70-year-old thatch was absolutely filthy, dry, old vegetation – it seemed like tons of the stuff. I was looking through the yellow pages, wondering if we could ever get a person to thatch it, when I found a company called Sharp, in Wokingham, offering five generations of thatching, right on our doorstep!

The senior member of the Sharp family came to size it and said, 'Oh yes, I've worked on this.' His son and his grandson did the thatching. They used hard, hollow water weed from the Camargue and the ridges are done in straw and cut into a pattern. The straw has to be netted to discourage the birds who can get at it for their nests. The water weed is too hard and uncomfortable for nesting material, but we do have a problem with magpies. They get up there and tug – they think the pieces of weed are worms.

Peter Colebrook I am not a great believer in ghosts but various people said they had seen a lady from time to time. She wore diaphanous nightclothes. I never had the pleasure of seeing her but my wife thought she did and so did the children.

Jenny Cuff My neighbour's brother-in-law is quite psychic and he met a little girl dressed in a green dress coming in here. There was nothing awful about it. It was just a sighting, a little girl in green.

Peter Colebrook We went back to the see the people at The Spinney about two years ago. Looking at it now from the outside, it is totally and utterly different from what it used to be, but once you are inside with that great hedge all round it, it is much the same. You don't really see the other houses.

Jenny Cuff When the Colebrooks came here for tea, Mrs Colebrook handed me a plastic bag and said: 'This belongs to you and it belongs to the house.' I opened it and there was a little Victorian chimney sweep's boot which they had found up the chimney when the fireplace was being renovated. She had kept the boot on her desk as a sign of good luck for years and she felt it was appropriate to bring it back. It sits on the mantelpiece and when we sell it will be a condition of selling that it remains there because it truly belongs to the house.

T&C Shoe Repairs, 237 Oxford Road

There is something reassuring about T&C Shoe Repairs shop, in Oxford Road. It makes no concessions to modern glossiness and is resolutely an old-fashioned shop which gets on with the serious business of repairs. It continues a long tradition, for there has been a bootmakers there since before the First World War. The shop was built in about 1905, on or near the site of the Tramway stables and depot, and Robert Cox, a boot repairer, was there for many years from about 1911. He was followed by Jack D Sym, also in the trade, and in 1972 the shop became Turners shoe repairs. Bob Turner still owns it although he has moved to Twyford and now rents the premises to Terry Rachford and Cliff Sopp (the T and C of the present name).

Claire
Nurse

The shop stands in a parade on the busy Oxford Road. 'The street has got busier and busier outside,' said Claire Nurse, who has worked in the shop for 12 years. 'If it wasn't for the island outside it would be very difficult to cross. You take your life in your hands when you cross that road – you have to be a good dodger.'

It's a three-storey building, with steep stairs leading to the rooms above. 'Many's the time I've pulled big sheets of rubber up there,' said Claire with feeling. 'Nobody else would bother! We don't use all of the floors. In one of the rooms upstairs, John does stitching and patching, and surgical work like raising heels and soles. There's a room for the book-keeper, and the rest of the rooms are used for storage. The third floor isn't used at all.'

The ground floor area is unexpectedly long and deep. In the back, busy with repairs, is Philip Goodship, who has been in the shoe repair trade for 40 years. He grew up in Connaught Road, and has always known the shop but it was not until 1993 that he came to work there.

'I started work when I was 14 as a shoe repairer at Mr Eggleton's, in Oxford Road, where the Butts Centre is now,' he said. 'It was difficult to get an apprenticeship then so I was a trainee. Since then I have worked in different heel bars and street bars in the town. Before I came here, I was nine years at the shoe repairers in School Road, Tilehurst, which I built up from scratch.'

Claire has noticed many changes since she came to shop in 1982. 'The shop was quite grandiose when I started. Bob sold leather goods and hides but fashion changed. It wasn't the right area to sell these expensive handbags so it gradually dropped out. It's mainly shoe repairs now, key cutting and sundries – we do very well on shoelaces!

'We have regulars who always pop in and we get people bringing in their old favourites which they like to get repaired even if it's quite a lot of money. One woman come in with a pair of riding boots and said: 'You always do them for me whatever state they're in.' You also get particular items, such as sports gloves to be reinforced with bits of leather.

'People come up here with jobs that the town can't do. It's "Oh, they sent me up here, you're the only people that can do this", because other repairers don't do difficult jobs. We have the monopoly on stitching.'

As if to prove her point, Paul Woodward, a regular customer from Reading, arrived to collect his walking boots which T&C had rebuilt for him with new insoles, a new middle and commando units.

'I've had these walking boots for about 15 years and I have travelled most of the western hemisphere and various bits of Europe in them,' he said. 'My dad bought them for me, and I've worn them ever since.

'They've taken me all over the place. Once I was in the Rockies camping, when I had a close shave with a bear. My boots were outside the tent and when the bear came into the camp, I left the tent one end and the boots were scattered round the other. We kept very still and luckily the bear just wandered off!'

Other customers are not so attached to their footwear. 'We have

T&C Shoe Repairs *drawn by Tammy Dodsworth*

Philip
Goodship

shoes on the shelves that go back one or two years and there's a row of boxes with old shoes that people have never collected which are probably four or five years old,' said Claire. 'I've just started putting them out to see if people will buy them.'

T&C does a lot of contract work now – 'It's more like a factory,' said Philip. It's part of Claire's job to collect and deliver from different shops, like hardware shops and newsagents, that want to take in shoe repairs for a bit of commission. They cover a big area, as far afield as Buckingham, and Claire can travel 190 miles on one of her rounds.

But the bread and butter work is still soles and heels. Philip used to time himself to see how fast he could do them but he doesn't bother now.

'We can't guarantee with man-made shoes how long they'll stick for, but we'll do our best,' said Claire. 'Even the manufacturer can't get their shoes to stick, so how can they expect us to do better?

'If people bring us shoes to be soled and heeled on a Saturday morning, they can collect them in the afternoon. A chappie came in this morning who wanted a pair of shoes done as he was going to wear them for a wedding this afternoon – I don't think he was the bridegroom!'

❦ *Bouquet* **The University Cloister, London Road**

Guiding a student to the Great Hall the other day I was struck by her charmed surprise at the peaceful beauty of the London Road campus. The university's sole home for the first half of this century, nowadays students may never see it until their graduation ceremony, for which the Great Hall is still used. The public see it perhaps only when there is a concert, or for evening classes. Otherwise it's left to the students of Gyosei College. The Japanese of all people surely appreciate the roofed cloisters with their heavy wooden supporting beams, surrounding lawns and a sunken garden with a gnarled mulberry. A recent touch is the international Friendship Gate looking through to a charming low fountain and beyond to the tulip tree in George Palmer's old garden. It is good to realize that the place still gives real pleasure in the present.
Dermot O'Rourke

The Town Hall

The Town Hall was originally the Assembly Rooms and included the room now known as the Victoria Hall. The façade, as we see it today, was added to the building in the 19th century by the renowned architect Alfred Waterhouse. Further additions were made in subsequent years, creating the Museum of Reading and the Concert Hall, all of which are undergoing a programme of extensive refurbishment. Plans to extend the Town Hall on its existing site were interrupted by the First World War. It was not until 1975 that the new civic offices were opened and since then the Town Hall complex has been impressively restored. Laura Milner has been manager of the Town Hall since August 1990.

The Town Hall stopped dealing with the civic functions of Reading in 1975, when the offices were moved to the new Civic Centre, but a number of functions were left here like the museum and the library. The building was literally gutted in about 1986 when everyone was moved out. One of the towers was replaced on the building, which rather confused people because they couldn't recall it ever having been there. The place was bombed during the Second World War and the tower had been missing for a number of years.

I was involved with the building before it was re-opened in 1989 as part of my work for the Head of Catering at Reading Borough Council, and when the Town Hall manager's job came up I was lucky enough to get it. My background is very practical. I started in the catering business and worked my way up the rungs from chief pot-washer – no, to be honest, bottom pot-washer – through to managerial responsibility. It's terribly difficult still for women to get into management. I have been very fortunate with Reading Borough Council, though, I have never felt I was a woman who was trying to prove something. I've always felt I was an employee like the rest of them and had capabilities that they were actually using. But it's much more difficult in the private sector.

Running a building of this size takes a lot of courage and a certain amount of insanity. Firstly, it helps to have a Rottweiler – everyone should have one. Mine is called Christine Johnson and she is my assistant manager who deals with many of the day-to-day issues in the building, and guards me with amazing ferocity from all those people wishing to sell us 'tampon machines equipped with a full year's supply', guaranteed to last all of five seconds after installation, or 'your business could benefit greatly by advertising in our monthly magazine on double glazing'.

We are also responsible for the 24-hour security of the Town Hall and Museum of Reading, and on many occasions have watched the dawn come up whilst awaiting an engineer to repair a faulty intruder detector.

The public face of the Town Hall is that of a beautifully-restored Victorian footprint on the landscape. It is our job to keep it like that. It is often very difficult not to get angry with the way some of our 'customers' abuse this service, and to remember that a great many people get much enjoyment from their visit to the Town Hall and Museum and pay respect to the service we offer.

There is no way that we can expect people to understand fully the complexities of keeping the bricks and mortar together nor, quite frankly should they need to. They should be able to visit the Town Hall and see a well-run building that is there for the benefit of everyone.

When I first came to Reading, I had a vision of it being a new town and perhaps slightly Birmingham-ish, not terribly attractive and probably a concrete jungle, but this is a beautiful part of the world. I come from Yorkshire and I feel that people do not think of their roots like they used to. Reading has many immigrant residents, not only from multi-ethnic cultures, but also from other parts of Britain and perhaps they do not see themselves as belonging here. There is a feeling of a 'civic heart' here but probably not enough.

People need to get a grip of what we've got here. The work that has been going on at this end of the town – the refurbishment of the Town Hall, a nice, new post office, national stores coming in like Long Tall Sally and Weatherspoons – is really brightening it up. New life is being breathed into the town.

George Fage is the official Town Crier for the town and district of Reading. He moved to Tilehurst two years ago when his wife inherited an Edwardian house. He is a Londoner, from Camden, and had been a greengrocer for 30 years in and around the West End until ill health forced him to retire 10 years ago. Now 65, George is the first Town Crier in Reading for 100 years.

For me, the difference between living in London and living in Reading is fantastic. I have lived in flats and just a few houses but never anything

Town Hall *drawn by Lynne Wilkes*

with a garden. I was always interested in flowers because I sold them in my greengrocer's shop, so to have a house with a garden – well, that was absolute heaven. If you live in Reading, and especially in what I call the suburbs of Reading, you don't realise how quiet it is. You may grumble about traffic and overhead noise from planes, but it is nothing like London. In London it is 24 hours a day, especially coming from where I do, an inner-city area.

One other curious thing I noticed – and it probably wouldn't occur to you – you can actually see the sky. Now, in London, you don't notice the sky, just the buildings, and I haven't seen stars for 40 years since I was a child. Even in Reading there's that glow, but even so I'm pleased to see the sky! And, of course, greenery – that's what you notice. Mostly I notice the quiet and how much cleaner it is, even though Camden and

George
Fage

Westminster areas have pulled their socks up and they are cleaner than they were.

When we came to Reading, I decided to do some research about town crying and discovered the Guild of Town Criers. So I joined it and learned quite a lot. Over the centuries Town Criers seem to have been a Jack-of-all-trades. They were a kind of night-watchman, walking round the town, and if they saw what we would call layabouts congregating, they would ring their bell and tell them to move on. They were empowered to arrest them and put them in the stocks, as well as being responsible for the boundaries and the fences.

When I moved to Tilehurst, we felt that we ought to get out and meet people. As Reading was seeking city status and I had previously done some town crying, I suggested I should become Town Crier. What you need for a town crier is a loud voice, good diction, a good bellringing arm and the facility to get on with people. The main job of the Town Crier originally was to pass on news from the Lord of the Manor or the Council, and international news such as the outbreak of war, and 'the French are invading!'— that sort of thing. It was how most country town people got their news. Nowadays, the Town Crier accompanies the Lord Mayor or other officials and attracts people's attention to whatever is going on.

I am very impressed with Reading and its borough council. Its services are good and there are a great deal of leisure activities going on, especially throughout the summer. If you have a family of youngsters, there's something on every weekend.

Reading is a mixture of the modern and the traditional. A bustling university town, with a thriving, progressive business culture, it deserves to be a city. Its greatest asset is its people. From experience, I know them to be very friendly and welcoming. It's a good place to live, work and raise a family. Although Reading has not had such a heroic past as some towns in the county, it has its own history of normal life and the common people. My impression is that Reading could beneficially attract more tourists by making more of what it's got.

The Triangular Houses of Cardigan Road

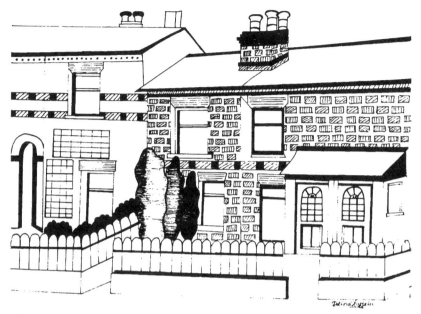

The Triangular Houses *drawn by Dolina Hussein*

Five parallel roads lead off the south of Addington Road, between Alexandra Road and Eastern Avenue. Hundreds of seemingly uniform terraced houses were built around 1881, so why single out No 82 Cardigan Road? Most houses are squares or rectangles, especially when the roads follow a gridiron pattern as these five do. But seen on an aerial photograph or a large-scale map, nos 82 and 84 are triangles.

Walking up the road you can see an obvious change at this point. Number 84 has a taller roof-line and more flamboyant brickwork, as have all the remaining houses on both sides of the road. But 82 has an unusually narrow frontage. The front garden is a 25 degree wedge which at the gate is only 55 inches. The present owner, Mr Sal Omar, had no idea why the house and garden were so oddly shaped. 'I bought the house for its large garden. I hope to encourage wildlife,' he said. But despite the great eucalyptus tree at the end, there are no koalas.

From a street frontage of less than five feet, the site widens so much that the back garden wall adjoins no fewer than six of the gardens of

Foxhill Road. When not gardening, Mr Omar is refurbishing the house to give a Victorian cottage feel to the place. Understandably he did the smaller front room first. In the back room he replaced defective skirting boards and they are so long that there was enough sound timber to use for an elaborate stripped pine mantelpiece.

A former owner of the triangular house, Edith Spencer, asked about the puzzling shape when she was young. 'Ours was once the last house in Reading,' her father told her. And there you have it. Up to 1887, when Reading was expanded to take in Whitley, the borough boundary took this diagonal course across the corner of the new Redlands estate, and no house could be built across it, or even part of a house – you can see where the corner of 100 Foxhill Road is bevelled to avoid encroachment.

There is a more subtle indicator of this boundary: outside No 82 the kerbstones change style, showing that the road once stopped there. This can be seen also in Foxhill Road, and again in Alexandra Road just above Lydford Road.

The houses up to No 82 were mostly built in 1881, certainly all by 1886. Beyond, in the hamlet of Whitley, were the wooded grounds of Foxhill House (distinct from Foxhill, in Whiteknights) which was demolished about 1895. By 1899 the roads were completed and joined at the top by Cardigan Gardens. A new triangular house adjoins the old one but is somehow less noticeable with its narrowing at the back. Moreover the road now bends slightly and the walls are angled so that all the gardens are about the same shape and size.

◻ *Brickbat* **Basingstoke Road Telephone Exchange**

Look from South Whitley towards Reading, arrow-straight up Northumberland Avenue, you see rising up the spire of Christchurch. Like a rocket - like a prayer they once would have said - reaching for the heavens. Dominating the horizon. Well, once it did. Now domination is given over to a great glass and concrete slab dedicated to Telecommunications. My hope is to live to see it demolished, its contents microminiaturised into a cupboard.

Dermot O'Rourke

Whitley Wood Supermarket and Handiy Store

Whitley Wood is a densely-populated part of Reading that really does have a wood, close to which the Whitley Wood Supermarket can be found. It is not quite the size of the new Safeway, in the Basingstoke Road, but it provides for all the day-to-day needs of the local community and it remains open seven days a week, from very early until late in the evening. The appetising, early morning smells from its self-contained bakery might suggest to strangers that they were in one of those old English villages where the baker sold you hot loaves in one piece instead of cold, sliced bread in a plastic cover.

Next door to the supermarket is the Handiy Store. No, that is not a spelling mistake but a good indication of the purpose served. On Sundays, the DIY dads pop along there for the odd tin of paint, tube of glue, or something from the huge selection of nails and screws that they forgot to stock up on before the weekend. Local children, too, can spend small amounts of pocket money on modest toys or small gifts for grandparents, and mothers can replenish anything from domestic utensils to stationery or cleaning equipment. The shop's photocopying service has got to be the cheapest in Reading.

This double resource has been developed by Mahesh Patel and his father, aided by assistants from the local community, all providing the kind of complete personal service that has almost disappeared.

Mahesh Patel I was born in Nairobi, my father was born in India and my mother in Mombasa. We lived in Kenya until 1963 when Kenya was granted independence. It was then that my parents decided to go to India. In India I was educated at an English school. It was in India that I acquired my Indian cultural knowledge. Then, in 1968, my parents once again decided to move home and this time it was to England. We arrived in Southall where I continued my education. While at school there in 1970, I remember going on a school trip – a Mediterranean cruise – where we were all thrown together on a ship for some 15 days and everyone accepted everyone else whatever their colour or culture.

As a Hindu, I am, of course, involved with the fellowship of the four to five hundred Hindu families in Reading. It would be nice if we could eventually have our own temple but one wonders whether the existing community is really large enough to support it. One aspect of our religion is that we do not have to go somewhere to a

Mahesh
Patel

designated building to practise and experience our particular faith. Our own homes can be our temples.

For relaxation on Sundays in the summer, we have organised a cricket team and play at Holme Park, Sonning. The majority of the players represent a very international assembly – West Indian, English Indian, Pakistani and South African. We enjoy this very English Sunday activity as a total contrast to our working week with the long hours of shop opening and service to the public.

When I was young and considering what I would like to be when I left school, I very much fancied a career as an RAF pilot. Unfortunately, I was not quite good enough to pass the test but was offered an alternative role as navigator, which did not really appeal to me. My father wanted me to be an accountant and now, as a partly qualified accountant, here I am in Whitley Wood running the shops and being part of the community.

The Patels represent a very close unit and section of the Indian community in Reading. They are not all members of the same family and have different lives, as four of Mahesh's friends explain.

Dil Patel I was born in this country and therefore educated here. Mahesh and I are from different generations and don't necessarily share the same philosophy or point of view. He relates much more to the traditions and culture of India, while I have a large circle of English friends and work in a white environment concerned with advertising. I consider myself much more Westernised and relate to Western customs and people. My children will be different again as our culture becomes even more diluted.

Harish Patel I find Reading a far better place than London where I used to live. Tilehurst is nice and clean and very friendly, and I have a very successful business there.

Umakant Patel As I have health problems and suffer from asthma, I chose to live higher up rather than down in Reading's lower valley areas. I, too, also have a shop there.

Gunvant Patel My shop is in Woodley, the cream of Reading! Like Harish, I moved from east London six years ago. We are all very happy in this area of Berkshire.